D1528493

UNDERSTANDING
JOHN UPDIKE

UNDERSTANDING CONTEMPORARY AMERICAN LITERATURE
Matthew J. Bruccoli, Founding Editor
Linda Wagner-Martin, Series Editor

UNDERSTANDING

JOHN UPDIKE

Frederic J. Svoboda

The University of South Carolina Press

© 2018 University of South Carolina

Published by the University of South Carolina Press
Columbia, South Carolina 29208

www.sc.edu/uscpress

Manufactured in the United States of America

27 26 25 24 23 22 21 20 19 18   10 9 8 7 6 5 4 3 2 1

Library of Congress Cataloging-in-Publication Data
can be found at http://catalog.loc.gov/.

ISBN: 978-1-61117-862-3 (hardcover)
ISBN: 978-1-61117-863-0 (ebook)

This book was printed on recycled paper with
30 percent postconsumer waste content.

In honor of Suzanne Henning Uphaus.
Among the first . . .

I cannot greatly care what critics say of my work; if it is good, it will come to the surface in a generation or two and float, and if not, it will sink, having in the meantime provided me with a living, the opportunities of leisure, and a craftsman's intimate satisfactions.

John Updike, *Conversations*

By his [Byron's] words he still lives. . . .

John Updike, *On Literary Biography*

CONTENTS

SERIES EDITOR'S PREFACE

The Understanding Contemporary American Literature series was founded by the estimable Matthew J. Bruccoli (1931–2008), who envisioned these volumes as guides or companions for students as well as good nonacademic readers, a legacy that will continue as new volumes are developed to fill in gaps among the nearly one hundred series volumes published to date and to embrace a host of new writers only now making their marks on our literature.

As Professor Bruccoli explained in his preface to the volumes he edited, because much influential contemporary literature makes special demands, "the word understanding in the titles was chosen deliberately. Many willing readers lack an adequate understanding of how contemporary literature works; that is, of what the author is attempting to express and the means by which it is conveyed." Aimed at fostering this understanding of good literature and good writers, the criticism and analysis in the series provide instruction in how to read certain contemporary writers—explicating their material, language, structures, themes, and perspectives— and facilitate a more profitable experience of the works under discussion.

In the twenty-first century Professor Bruccoli's prescience gives us an avenue to publish expert critiques of significant contemporary American writing. The series continues to map the literary landscape and to provide both instruction and enjoyment. Future volumes will seek to introduce new voices alongside canonized favorites, to chronicle the changing literature of our times, and to remain, as Professor Bruccoli conceived, contemporary in the best sense of the word.

Linda Wagner-Martin, Series Editor

PREFACE

John Updike died in January 2009, and with the end of his life came the opportunity to look back over a completed career and to sort out what was essential in his work from what garnered peripheral comments from critics and the public. A revaluation is appropriate, and the format of the Understanding Contemporary American Literature series allows scope for this undertaking as well as providing a forum that will reach both beginning students of the author as well as those who have long appreciated Updike's unique vision of American life.

One of the burdens—or perquisites—of authorial success is celebrity. It is a burden that Updike carried with considerable grace, aided by a modest, unassuming personality. As possible parallels, the public reputations of Mark Twain and Ernest Hemingway come to mind, one reputation fostering and the other detracting from appreciation of the real merits of these two seminal American novelists. Neither is quite a model for considering Updike, nor is the celebrity of his contemporary Norman Mailer, a force of nature and culture whose fiction did not always measure up to the outsized claims of his personality but who shaped the conversation of his time via his audaciously personal nonfiction; his role in founding the *Village Voice*, a newspaper of importance in the life of the nation; his celebrity life; and the larger-than-life gestures he made in the service of celebrity and his personal demons.

Probably Philip Roth (almost precisely Updike's contemporary, born one year later) is Updike's chief rival in appealing to a wide audience—both literate and popular—while garnering critical acclaim and simultaneously serving as a major figure in American culture and its criticism from just after the mid-twentieth century onward. Like Updike, Roth is an author whose body of work is likely to endure. These two authors are hardly identical in background or point of view, but they maintained a relationship as "friends at a distance" (Roth's phrase) for much of their professional lives. Claudia Roth Pierpont characterized their contrasting gifts as like those of the modernist painters Pablo Picasso and Henri Matisse: "Roth would have to be Picasso—the energy, the slashing power—and Updike would be Matisse: the color, the sensuality. . . .

Updike was the painter in words . . . Roth the master of voices. . . . But they are united in having spent a lifetime possessed by America" (303).

What Updike has left readers will endure beyond his obvious importance in his own time. He has his own author society and journal, the *John Updike Review,* which debuted in 2011 under the direction of James Schiff. The John Updike Society, led by James Plath, has sponsored several conferences and even has supported the purchase and ongoing restoration to its original condition of Updike's childhood home in Shillington, Pennsylvania. Adam Begley's magisterial biography of Updike appeared in 2014, preceded a year earlier by Jack De Bellis's *John Updike's Early Years* and Bob Batchelor's *John Updike: A Critical Biography.*

A difficulty of dealing with an author so prolific and multitalented as Updike is simply fitting discussion of him into a work of reasonable length. Thus, for the purposes of this study, it has been best to be selective. After a brief overview of his career, this work focuses primarily on Updike's book-length fiction, delving particularly into works that typify his interests and strengths: the four novels and one novella featuring Rabbit Angstrom, his excellent short fiction, the bestseller *Couples,* the five novels indebted to Nathaniel Hawthorne's *The Scarlet Letter,* and the satirical Henry Bech collections. His excellent short fiction is also considered. These related works demonstrate continuing strands in his fiction. Each major division in this study should stand alone for readers dipping into Updike's oeuvre. Additionally several sections suggest how Updike's works fit into specific elements forming the context of his time.

The reader should find herein not just an analysis but also an evocation of the pleasure of reading Updike. He was not only a significant author but also one who provided immense entertainment to readers of his time. Early in this project, I went to lunch with two married friends, Bob Uphaus and Lois Rosen, retired English professors, and let them know what I was working on. (Bob's late first wife, Suzanne, was an early scholar of Updike, and this book is dedicated in memory of her achievement.) "Oh, Updike!" Lois said. "You must be having a wonderful time." Their positive reactions were immediate and spontaneous—and provided a clear sense of how so many people experienced Updike's work throughout his career. Both are skilled and sophisticated readers, yet also fans.

An author who can produce such reactions is certainly worth our attention.

CHAPTER 1

Understanding John Updike

John Updike (1932–2009) was one of the most prolific, wide-ranging, and respected of twentieth-century American novelists, winner of every award available to an American writer, including the Pulitzer Prize (twice), the O. Henry Prize (twice), the National Book Critics Circle Award (three times), the National Book Award, and the PEN/Faulkner Award, to name only a few. Only the Nobel Prize for Literature eluded him. During his working life, he published at the rate of more than one book per year, more than sixty in all, including twenty-six novels and novellas and more than a dozen collections of short fiction. He was equally distinguished as a reviewer of literature and the fine arts, cultural critic, and poet. His career included a long-term association with two continuing American cultural treasures, the *New Yorker* (where much of his short fiction appeared) and the *New York Review of Books* (where he was a reviewer).

Early biography provides important keys to understanding his works and concerns. Updike was born on March 18, 1932, in rural West Reading, Pennsylvania. His father, Wesley Russell Updike, worked as a high school math teacher at Shillington High School (and later served as the model for the teacher protagonist in his son's early novel *The Centaur*); his mother, Linda Grace Hoyer Updike, was a clerk in a local department store but also a serious, though not entirely successful, writer who did eventually publish short fiction in the *New Yorker*. West Reading became the fictional setting of Brewer and nearby Shillington the fictional Olinger in John Updike's later works, and these places helped to form his subject matter.

"My subject is the American Protestant small town middle class. I like middles. It is in middles that extremes clash, where ambiguity restlessly rules,"

Updike told *Life* magazine reporter Jane Howard in 1966, suggesting something not only of his subject matter but also of the approach that informs his best work: the appreciation and understanding of ambiguity that made him such a perceptive writer.

Updike early hoped to become a cartoonist, and when he went to Harvard on scholarship as an English major, he worked on its noted campus humor magazine, the *Harvard Lampoon*. The *Lampoon* had been a considerable part of the appeal of Harvard to him. He served as its editor during his senior year and was prolific in producing prose and cartoons for the magazine. (He had followed a similar model during his high school career.)

Before graduating he married Mary Pennington, a Radcliffe College student of the fine arts. (At the time Harvard was not formally coeducational, but Radcliffe served as its associated women's school.) This first marriage provided the Updikes with four children—and the basis for his bittersweet and tender Maples stories, generally considered to be among his finest achievements in chronicling the state of American matrimony in the midcentury, which was an important continuing concern for Updike.

Graduating summa cum laude from Harvard in 1954, Updike won a fellowship for graduate work at Oxford University's Ruskin School of Drawing and Fine Art and studied in England until mid-1955. Connections made there with humorist James Thurber, Irish novelist Joyce Cary, and essayist E. B. White and his wife, Katherine White (fiction editor of the *New Yorker*), led him to New York City later that year and work on the *New Yorker*, particularly its famous "Talk of the Town" feature. His association with the magazine endured: it had a right of first refusal on his works and published hundreds of his stories, essays, and reviews over the course of his life.

There is a certain irony here in that the magazine's founding editor, Harold Ross, famously had proclaimed that "*The New Yorker* will be the magazine which is not edited for the old lady from Dubuque"—the magazine for sophisticates, not the ordinary American. However, in his *Paris Review* interview of 1967, Updike suggested a seemingly conflicting goal: "Hemingway described literary New York as a bottle full of tapeworms trying to feed on each other. When I write, I aim in my mind not toward New York but toward a vague spot a little to the east of Kansas. I think of the books on library shelves, without their jackets, years old, and a countryish teenaged boy finding them, have them speak to him. The reviews, the stacks in Brentano's [book store], are just hurdles to get over, to place the books on that shelf."

Here as elsewhere it is clear that Updike was aware of his literary forebears but also intent on setting his own course. Throughout his career he navigated successfully between sophisticated and mass audience appeal. The "countryish teenaged boy" of the quotation recalls Updike's personal roots as well, particularly the sandstone farmhouse to which his parents had moved in 1945 when he was thirteen, dislocating him from comfortable town life (Begley 32), a setting that figures memorably in a number of his short stories.

By 1957 the Updikes already had a son and a daughter, but Updike chose to leave his secure *New Yorker* position and move to Ipswich, Massachusetts (near the Atlantic coast on Ipswich Bay, about thirty miles north-northeast of Boston), and make his living as a freelance professional author. Then as now, Ipswich was both a Boston bedroom community for commuters and a summer resort. It served as model for the fictional Tarbox of the scandalous and hugely popular *Couples* (1968), set during the end of the Kennedy administration, and more or less for the fictional Eastwick, Connecticut, in the seriocomic *The Witches of Eastwick* (1984), set in 1968–69, which partly reflects Updike's reactions to the rise of women's consciousness at that time.

By 1958 Updike had published his first book, *The Carpentered Hen and Other Tame Creatures,* poems of considerable charm that, like his subsequent poetry, do not evince the same seriousness, and have not attracted the same level of interest, as his fiction. (In all these poems, however, one can see the author seriously at play with language, a continuing strength of Updike, who was a noted stylist.)

In the next year, Updike published both his first novel, *The Poorhouse Fair,* and his first collection of short stories, *The Same Door,* with Alfred A. Knopf, which firm would remain his American publishers for the rest of his career. A Solomon Guggenheim Foundation Fellowship supported work on what became the novel *Rabbit, Run,* his first breakout hit.

The Rabbit tetralogy is often considered as Updike's greatest achievement: *Rabbit, Run* (1960), *Rabbit Redux* (1971), *Rabbit Is Rich* (1981), and *Rabbit at Rest* (1990)—plus a fifth work, the novella *Rabbit Remembered* (2001), concerned with the family members left behind by the death of the books' protagonist. This saga of the life of an ordinary young man from small-town Pennsylvania traces the high point and fall of midcentury American self-confidence and energy through Harry "Rabbit" Angstrom, who achieves his own high point quite early in life—as a high school basketball star. From that point onward, Rabbit finds marriage, fatherhood, love affairs, work, and even monetary success as proprietor of a Toyota dealership not quite to be what he is longing for. His perpetual searching makes Rabbit fully human and engaging despite his many flaws; in his longings and worries, he re-creates the American state of mind over the mid to late twentieth century.

As in much of Updike, the Rabbit books brilliantly render the physical surfaces of American life, but they also reveal the currents beneath those surfaces.

Rabbit is *l'homme moyen sensual,* perhaps, in the sense meant by Justice John M. Woolsey of the U.S. District Court of New York in his famous 1933 opinion, later affirmed by the Supreme Court, lifting the ban on James Joyce's *Ulysses* and laying the groundwork for Updike's eventual exploration of previously proscribed areas of human experience. Rabbit is an ordinary sensual man, not well educated, yet still with considerable insight into his own life in small-town America, which is exquisitely rendered both in the novels' present time and in Rabbit's memories of the lost America of his childhood. A part of Updike's genius lies in his ability to write within the limitations of perception of such a character yet to let his greater authorial perception plausibly shine through. He is always a master of point of view. As one example, in the final novel, *Rabbit at Rest,* the loss of a huge copper beech tree that once shaded the old house that Rabbit shares with his wife and mother-in-law becomes as eloquently evocative to Rabbit as the remembered sacrifices of World War II, and Updike makes readers consider how much even a very ordinary man may perceive.

By the early 1960s, Updike's career was well launched. Stories had appeared multiple times in *The Best American Short Stories* volumes ("A Gift from the City" in 1959; the much-anthologized meditation on mortality "Pigeon Feathers" in 1962) and in the *O Henry Prize Stories* ("The Doctor's Wife" in 1962). His novel *The Poorhouse Fair* won the Rosenthal Award of the National Institute of Arts and Letters in 1960, and *The Centaur* (1963) won the National Book Award in that same year. Additional collections of stories (*Pigeon Feathers,* 1962) and poetry (*Telephone Poles and Other Poems,* 1963) also appeared. From this point on, a complete listing even of his book publications becomes more a matter for a bibliography than for this brief biographical and critical essay, and so a selective approach was taken.

Further, in 1964 Updike was elected as one of the 250 members of the National Institute of Arts and Letters. He was one of the youngest ever chosen by this group, founded in 1904 and including over the years such luminaries as Henry James, Edith Wharton, John Dos Passos, John Singer Sergeant, Theodore Roosevelt, Carl Sandberg, Ezra Pound, Archibald MacLeish, Mark Rothko, and Charles Dana Gibson. (Updike's nearer contemporaries in the institute included Allen Ginsberg, Kurt Vonnegut Jr., and Mary McCarthy.) In 1976 he was elected to the fifty-member American Academy of Arts and Letters, then a more selective subgroup of the National Institute. Among earlier members the critic, editor and novelist William Dean Howells would probably come closest to modeling Updike's importance as a widely influential, even beloved cultural arbiter.

Also in 1964 Updike traveled to Eastern Europe and the Soviet Union as a cultural ambassador under the auspices of the U.S. Department of State, gaining experiences later adapted into some of the highly satirical Henry Bech stories and novellas, about a hack Jewish novelist striving to rise in the literary world. These works also incorporate some of Updike's other experiences as a member of the nation's official cultural elite and let him comment rather directly on the profession of authorship. Updike also made a foray into writing for children in the early to mid-1960s, with *The Magic Flute* (1962), *Bottom's Dream* (1965), and *A Child's Calendar* (1965).

Through the rest of the 1960s, Updike published several novels, his first collection of essays (*Assorted Prose*, 1965), another collection of verse, and three more stories in the O. *Henry Prize Stories* ("The Music School" in 1966; "Marching through Boston" in 1967, the latter reflecting the author's participation in a Boston civil rights march; and "Your Lover Just Called" in 1968). The latter two are Maples stories; all three treat problems of marital relationships in affluent postwar America.

His 1968 novel *Couples* was a huge commercial success, staying on the best-seller lists for a year, earning a substantial movie advance payment, and leading to Updike's first appearance on the cover of the influential weekly newsmagazine *Time*, his portrait accompanied by the headline "The Adulterous Society." This book is sometimes down-rated for its treatment of adultery and wife-swapping among ten suburban couples but in fact is a work of considerable insight as well as technical achievement in narration, keeping its many characters in play throughout.

The protagonist of *Couples*, a Dutch American contractor born in western Michigan, Piet Hannema, is a more thoughtful and appealing Rabbit in some ways, though also a sensual man, but his last name further suggests anima, soul, and the deeper spiritual implications of midcentury affluence and success. Like Updike, Piet is a seeker after religious faith (and unlike Updike ultimately a failed one), but in any case he is a protagonist facing head-on midcentury America's dilemma: attempting to reconcile affluent success with the fading of the religious values that once held the nation together—and with the loss of American innocence. The assassination of John F. Kennedy is the major historical event at the center of the book's chronology, one among a number of such events that place the book clearly in its place and time. *Couples* is a major novel and a part of Updike's continuing legacy.

In 1970 appeared *Bech: A Book*, a humorous hybrid of novella and short story collection that satirizes both the authorial struggle to succeed and then maintain a reputation and the careers of several of the Jewish American novelists who were the Protestant Updike's contemporaries. Updike returned to his alter ego Henry Bech in subsequent volumes in 1982 and 1998, with the satire becoming broader and perhaps more farfetched. Critical reaction to these books was mixed. They somewhat recall what British novelist Graham Greene had called "entertainments," books intended to be less serious and more overtly entertaining than that novelist's full-fledged works, but they do have serious points to make.

Rabbit Redux, which appeared in 1971 to considerable acclaim, reflects the events of the later sixties as *Couples* reflects the decade's earlier years. In the next year appeared *Seventy Poems* and the very distinguished *Museums and Women and Other Stories*. In 1973 Updike again was serving as a cultural ambassador—this time to nations in Africa—on a Fulbright Foundation–sponsored tour. This took him to Ghana, Nigeria, Kenya, Tanzania, and Ethiopia and energized and provided background for later novels, including *The Coup* (1978), *Terrorist* (2006), and perhaps even indirectly *Brazil* (1994), which also drew on a brief trip to that country.

In 1974 Updike published a play, *Buchanan Dying*, following in the unsuccessful steps of previous American novelists who attempted to make a move into the lucrative theater market, including Henry James and F. Scott Fitzgerald. Updike in his preface seemed to intimate that this very long work might not be much performed ("Were this play ever to be produced," he wrote), but it was several times in abridged form, first at Lancaster's Franklin and Marshall College two years after publication, with the fact that President James Buchanan was born nearby perhaps contributing to local interest in the play. This work also suggests another continuing Updike interest, the public personality seen in the context of his own time, to which he returned most notably in *Memories of the Ford Administration* (1993), in which a historian tells his own life's tale while simultaneously comparing thirty-eighth president Gerald Ford to James Buchanan, the fifteenth. Buchanan was the president immediately preceding Abraham Lincoln and is widely regarded as one of the worst, having done nothing to stem the South's movement toward secession, which flowered in the months between Lincoln's election and inauguration. During his administration Ford was similarly viewed by many, though since his reputation has risen, largely for his role in asserting the decency of the American presidency in the aftermath of the 1974 resignation of Richard M. Nixon. With Updike, subject matter seems seldom lost: throughout his career he returned to and reworked previous concerns adeptly and almost always to good effect. In the same year the author separated from his first wife, and the next year appeared another O. Henry Prize story, "Nakedness."

The novel *A Month of Sundays* also appeared in 1975, beginning a thematic concern with Puritan America and Nathaniel Hawthorne's masterful re-creation of it, particularly in his 1850 novel *The Scarlet Letter*. Updike's *A Month of Sundays* was a reenvisioning of the adulterous minister character of

The Scarlet Letter, Arthur Dimmesdale, and has generally been seen as forming a trilogy along with *Roger's Version* (1986), which deals with a modern-day version of Roger Chillingworth, Dimmesdale's nemesis, and *S.* (1988), a comic novel from the point of view of a decidedly modern version of Hester Prynne, Dimmesdale's lover. However, the seriocomic *The Witches of Eastwick* (1984) and its late-career sequel, *The Widows of Eastwick* (2008), are recognizably in the same line of inquiry into traditional American values and their limits (as well as the place of women in American society) and will be discussed in detail later along with the trilogy. *The Witches of Eastwick* is another of Updike's major achievements.

The essay collection *Picked-Up Pieces* (1975) was particularly notable for Updike's statement of his five or six principles for ethical reviewing of literature, also generally applicable to other arts. Briefly condensed, these are

1. Try to understand what the author wished to do, and do not blame him for not achieving what he did not attempt;
2. Give him enough direct quotation . . . so the review's reader can form his own impression;
3. Confirm your description of the book with quotation from the book;
4. Go easy on plot summary, and do not give away the ending;
5. If the book is judged deficient, cite a successful example along the same lines, from the author's oeuvre or elsewhere;

   Do not accept for review a book you are predisposed to dislike, or committed by friendship to like.

These principles go a long way toward explaining why Updike was so successful—and so sought out—as a reviewer. They are good-humored, sensible, and appealingly modest, traits shared by much of the author's best writing, whether in essay, fiction, or poetry. Incidentally this book attempts to follow the spirit of these principles in discussing the shape of his career and concerns and what he achieved in individual works.

Marry Me: A Romance appeared in 1976. It was seen at the time as reworking the themes of *Couples* less successfully than the earlier novel, perhaps inspired by the end of Updike's marriage. Adam Begley's recent biography of Updike reveals that it in fact was a prototype for *Couples,* written years earlier, in 1964. Updike remarried, to Martha Ruggles Bernhard, in 1977. After living in Georgetown, five years later the couple moved to a mansion in Beverly Farms, Massachusetts, where they resided for the rest of his life.

In 1979 the NBC television network broadcast an adaptation of the Maples stories titled *Too Far to Go,* and "The Music School" was adapted by the BBC the following year. Another story, "Gesturing," appeared in the 1980 *Best American Short Stories* anthology. In 1981 the third and most successful (and perhaps best) Rabbit novel, *Rabbit Is Rich,* appeared. It won major literary prizes, including the National Book Critics Circle Award, the American Book Award, and the Pulitzer Prize. Another *Best American Short Stories* selection, "Still of Some Use," worked with material similar to that of the Maples stories. The following year, *Bech Is Back* was published, and Updike again appeared on the cover of *Time,* with a pastel-hued portrait and a headline that proclaimed him to be "Going Great at 50."

A second National Book Critics Circle Award, this time for criticism, was won by *Hugging the Shore,* a collection of articles and reviews, in 1983. Also in that year, stories appeared in the anthologies *Best American Short Stories* ("Deaths of Distant Friends") and *O. Henry Prize Stories* ("The City").

The Witches of Eastwick continued Updike's thematic concern with Hawthorne, early American Puritan values, and their fallout in the twentieth century, first seen in *A Month of Sundays.* This satirical novel proved highly popular but also somewhat controversial because of its treatment of women seeking power through black magic. Not all readers at the time were amused, though the novel has gained stature in the years following its publication. The movie version, which departs significantly from the structure and events of the novel, is the most successful adaptation of Updike's work to date.

In 1985 another of Updike's stories, "The Other," was awarded an O. Henry Prize, and he also published the poetry collection *Facing Nature.*

Roger's Version appeared in 1986 and *S.* in 1988, completing (with the late exception of *The Widows of Eastwick*) Updike's explorations of the themes of Nathaniel Hawthorne. In the intervening year, 1987, came a collection of short stories, *Trust Me,* and the release of the film version of *The Witches of East-wick,* starring Cher, Michelle Pfeiffer, Susan Sarandon, and Jack Nicholson.

In 1988 Updike's story "Pigeon Feathers" was adapted for the PBS *American Playhouse* anthology series. That same year Updike was honored by a life achievement award from Brandeis University and gave the PEN/Malamud Memorial Reading at Washington, D.C.'s Folger Shakespeare Library. These highly prestigious recognitions preceded his receiving the National Medal of Arts from President George H. W. Bush in a White House ceremony in 1989. Established by Congress in 1984, the medal is awarded yearly to up to twelve artists and sponsors of the arts. The only fiction writers that preceded Updike as recipients are Ralph Ellison, Eudora Welty, Robert Penn Warren, and Saul Bellow, suggesting his apotheosis as a member of the American cultural elite. Also in 1989 Updike published the memoir *Self-Consciousness* as well as *Just Looking,* a collection of essays on art that demonstrates that he was a perceptive and accessible critic throughout his career.

Rabbit at Rest, the final full-length novel of the Rabbit series, appeared in 1990, bringing the protagonist's life to an end on an inner-city basketball court and thus ironically recalling his only moments of real glory as a high school sports hero. Together the Rabbit works are an exploration of the changing state of the ordinary American mind over a period of some three decades. *Rabbit at Rest* was another triumph, again winning Updike the National Book Critics Circle Award and the Pulitzer Prize for fiction. (He thus joined William Faulkner and Booth Tarkington as the only fiction writers to have won the Pulitzer on two different occasions.)

In the early 1990s, Updike continued to publish regularly and earn accolades. "A Sandstone Farmhouse," a story drawn from his early life, appeared in both the *Best American Short Stories* and *O. Henry Prize Stories* (winning first prize) anthologies in 1991. Another essay collection, *Odd Jobs,* was also published that year. *Memories of the Ford Administration,* another novel closely tied to a particular time and place (and a particular president), appeared in 1992. That year Updike also received an honorary doctor of letters degree from his alma mater, Harvard. In 1993 *Collected Poems, 1953–1993* was published. It was also a year in which Updike received both the highly prestigious Common Wealth Award for literary achievement and Key West, Florida's irreverent Conch Republic Prize for Literature, with a citation declaring that his work reflected the "daring and creative spirit of the Keys."

The novel *Brazil,* published in 1994, tells a magic-realist version of the story of legendary lovers Tristan and Isolde in a fantastical South American landscape. The novel cuts loose from the present to drift as far back as the time of the conquistadores before returning to modern Brazil. Also in 1994 Updike published *The Afterlife and Other Stories.*

In 1995 Updike received the William Dean Howells Medal from the American Academy of Arts and Letters. The award suggests that his place in the cultural life of the United States is on the level of the famous Howells, a novelist, promoter of literary realism, essayist, editor of the *Atlantic Monthly* and later *Harper's,* and friend of and advocate for other writers ranging from Mark Twain to Henry James. That same year Updike was named a Commandeur de l'Ordre des Arts et des Lettres by the government of France.

In the Beauty of the Lilies was published in 1996 and won the Ambassador Book Award for fiction presented by the English-Speaking Union, an originally British organization founded in 1918, now with branches worldwide to promote "the mutual advancement of education of the English-speaking peoples of the world." The novel, likely influenced in its form and subject matter by

E. L. Doctorow's *Ragtime* (1975), traces four generations of an American family, roughly 1910 to 1990, exploring a loss of religious faith and the rise of Hollywood as a center for America's new spiritual aspirations. In the first generation, a middle-aged minister in Paterson, New Jersey, loses his faith and leaves his congregation, to the detriment of his family; by the fourth generation, an aimless young man joins a commune and dies thwarting a massacre like the one that killed the Branch Davidians in 1993, in a siege by federal agents in which leader David Koresh, at least eighty-two followers, and four government agents eventually died.

The science-fiction novel *Toward the End of Time* appeared in 1997 to mixed reviews. It traces the aftermath of a Chinese-U.S. nuclear war in the year 2020 from the point of view of an irascible and unpleasant retired investment adviser facing his own mortality. Updike's comical Jewish alter ego, Henry Bech, returned the next year in *Bech at Bay: A Quasi-Novel*. Harvard honored Updike again in 1998, awarding him the fourth Harvard Arts Medal, founded in 1995 to recognize "a distinguished Harvard alumnus or Radcliffe alumna or faculty member who has achieved excellence in the arts and who has made a special contribution to the public good or education, broadly defined." His predecessors as recipients were actor Jack Lemmon and singers Pete Seeger and Bonnie Raitt. *More Matter*, another collection of essays, appeared in 1999.

In 2000 appeared two considerable works, *Gertrude and Claudius* and *Licks of Love: Short Stories and a Sequel, "Rabbit Remembered,"* and the modest but graceful *On Literary Biography*. *Gertrude and Claudius* is essentially a prequel to William Shakespeare's *Hamlet*, drawing on that play and on the Bard's own source material. *Licks of Love* collects short stories on the topic of love, most not of the first rank of Updike's work, but it includes the novella *Rabbit Remembered*, which returns once more to the life of Rabbit Angstrom, seeing him from the point of view of his family members roughly a decade after his death. Particularly the novella presents the point of view of Rabbit's son Nelson, whose life never measured up to that of his father but who finally achieves maturity. *On Literary Biography*, a short, limited edition, reflects the author's belief that literary biography is a secondary art, that only the creative work can make even the life of so colorful a character as Lord Byron of interest to readers.

A new collection of poems, *Americana*, appeared in 2001. It was followed by *Seek My Face* (2002), which, like the early novel *The Poorhouse Fair*, is set during a single day. Its protagonist, a successful painter in the twilight of her years, talks at length to a young female interviewer about her life, her art, and her marriages to two famous artists in an exploration of the role of artistic experimentation in the mid-twentieth century. (The first husband is a lightly fictionalized version of abstract expressionist Jackson Pollock, and the second is an amalgamation of pop art stars including Andy Warhol.) Updike in an author's note acknowledged his debt to the life story of Pollock and his wife, Lee Miller. Like *The Witches of Eastwick,* this novel was an attempt to plumb a female protagonist, largely successful but marred perhaps by too-excessive reliance on its source material.

The collection *The Early Stories: 1953–1975* appeared in 2003, and Updike was awarded the National Humanities Medal. In 2004 the novel *Villages* (2004) was published. It traces computer programmer and pioneer Owen Mackenzie's life in three successive villages in Pennsylvania, Connecticut, and Massachusetts (representing boyhood, adulthood, and old age), somewhat recalling the Rabbit tetralogy and *Couples* in its themes of middle American angst, seeking, and sensuality over time. Alternating chapters explore the sexuality of the protagonist. The following year another collection of essays on art, *Still Looking,* was published.

Terrorist (2006) takes on post-9/11 American fear in the person of an Arab American Islamic teenager who searches for meaning in what to him seems an increasingly secularized America, largely represented by his high school in a fictionalized, decaying Paterson, New Jersey. He is redeemed via the efforts of his self-doubting, Rabbit-like high school guidance counselor, who rides along with him in his suicide-bomb-rigged truck and convinces him not to blow up the Lincoln Tunnel. The novel was a best-seller, widely (though not always positively) reviewed, and the subject of a major publicity campaign on the part of Updike and his publisher. In this year Updike also received the Rea Award for the Short Story, intended to honor originality and influence on the genre overall rather than any particular work, in essence a career achievement award. Jurors for 2006 were the distinguished fiction writers Ann Beattie, Richard Ford, and Joyce Carol Oates, all previous winners of the award, as were Alice Munro, Eudora Welty, and Cynthia Ozick.

The last novel published in Updike's lifetime was *The Widows of Eastwick* (2008). This sequel revisits the three now-aged protagonists of *The Witches of Eastwick,* remarried and then widowed in the years since the earlier novel, as they travel the world, return to Eastwick, and face their own mortality.

Updike died of lung cancer on January 27, 2009, in Danvers, Massachusetts. His death was followed that summer by the publication of two story collections: *My Father's Tears and Other Stories,* which collects stories concerned with aging and mortality from the last decade of the author's life, and the distinguished *The Maples Stories,* which assembles eighteen short stories of younger married life published previously in other collections. *New York Times* reviewer Michiko Kakutani characterized *My Father's Tears* "as a perfect bookend to 'Pigeon Feathers,' the precocious collection of stories that nearly five

decades ago announced their 30-year-old writer's discovery of his own inimi-
table voice."

Obituaries and other responses to Updike's passing underlined his importance to the novel and to the cultural life of the United States. Almost all were
strongly laudatory, if sometimes quirky in tone, though the *Times Literary
Supplement* took the occasion to republish expatriate American novelist Gore
Vidal's negative review of *In the Beauty of the Lilies* from 1996, in which he
took Updike to task for supposed middle-American ignorance of the larger
world. But more representative were the words of Philip Roth: "John Updike is
our time's greatest man of letters, as brilliant a literary critic and essayist as he
was a novelist and short story writer. He is and always will be no less a national
treasure than his 19th-century precursor, Nathaniel Hawthorne."

CHAPTER 2

The Rabbit Angstrom Tetralogy

Updike's Masterpiece and Template
for Understanding His Works

Generally acknowledged as Updike's greatest achievement, the Rabbit Angstrom books appeared roughly one per decade beginning in 1960. What is generally termed the Rabbit Tetralogy comprises *Rabbit, Run* (1960), *Rabbit Redux* (1971), *Rabbit Is Rich* (1981), and *Rabbit at Rest* (1990) plus a novella, *Rabbit Remembered,* published in the story collection *Licks of Love* (2001). The hero of the series, if he may be called that, is a somewhat gormless man, Harry Angstrom (nicknamed "Rabbit"), who hit the high point of his life as a high school basketball star in 1950s America and whose subsequent misadventures trace the fall of his—and American—preeminence through the late twentieth century. Understanding the strengths, weaknesses, and appeal of these books goes a long way toward helping to understand John Updike's general appeal and importance.

Rabbit shares all the weaknesses and prejudices of his times. He is a contemporary of the author himself who shares many of Updike's concerns but not his insight or grace, save perhaps in the physical sense of Rabbit's early athleticism. His progress from hapless young married man in small-town Pennsylvania through the tumult of the 1960s, the loss of his industrial economy job as a Linotype operator, and then contented middle age as a Toyota dealer leads to a heart attack on an inner-city basketball court in his mid-fifties when he unwisely goes one-on-one with a young black athlete in the last act of what was a lifelong attempt somehow to recapture his long-past glory. *Rabbit Remembered* examines his legacy, ten years after his death, particularly in the persons of his son and wife. Son Nelson is an even more hapless character than Rabbit, and he manages to lose the family's Toyota franchise through embezzlement fueled by drug addiction. In *Rabbit, Run* Rabbit's long-suffering, highly limited wife, Janice, accidentally drowns their infant daughter in the bathtub while drunk, after Rabbit temporarily leaves her for another woman, who bears him an illegitimate daughter. Both women are important characters in the series.

Rabbit's connections to the main currents of American history and culture as well as Updike's ability to evoke specific times and places make the series evocative for a wide range of readers. Despite the character's casual misogyny, racism, fear of responsibility, and general cluelessness, there is something appealing to many readers in Rabbit's improbable optimism, as well as in his ability to bounce back from each seeming comeuppance. An early inspiration for the series came from Harvard literature professor Harry Levin, who taught Updike in courses that covered a range of authors, including Shakespeare, Thomas Mann, James Joyce, and Marcel Proust. According to Jack De Bellis, Updike "never forgot Levin's remark in a Shakespeare course that fortified Updike's concern for average people: "Shakespeare's characters have no I.Q.s'" (*Updike Encyclopedia* 197). Though an ordinary character, Rabbit still reflects his time and mirrors the concerns of his countrymen. As Updike explained in a 1981 mock interview conducted by his character and writerly alter ego, Henry Bech, his aim was "bringing the corners forward. Or throwing light into them, if you'd rather. Singing the hitherto unsung. . . . I distrust books involving spectacular people, or spectacular events. Let *People* and *The National Enquirer* pander to our taste for the extraordinary; let literature concern itself, as the Gospels do, with the inner lives of hidden men."

Updike's choice of focus was sometimes a source of controversy, most notably among feminists in the late 1960s and 1970s. Rabbit's cluelessness extends to his treatment of the females around him, and whether Updike shared his creation's sexism remained an open question during his career, with respect to the female characters in the Rabbit books as well as in other later works.

Updike's subject matter is the middle class, specifically men leading ordinary, quotidian lives, which places him as part of several traditions of American literature. Like the novelist Sinclair Lewis (1885–1951), Updike is a realist whose fiction is so well observed as sometimes to move almost imperceptibly into satire even in his more serious works. Unlike Lewis, however, he always seems highly conscious of the ironies of the material he is presenting. Lewis's most famous character, boosterish real-estate agent George Follansbee Babbitt, is recalled in Rabbit Angstrom, and a quotation from Lewis serves as an epigraph in the two-volume collection *The Rabbit Novels:* "At night he [Babbitt] lights up a good cigar, and climbs into the little old 'bus, and maybe cusses the carburetor, and shoots out home. He mows the lawn, or sneaks in some practice putting, and then he's ready for dinner." Rabbit is often as crass as Babbitt and as ordinary and also is inarticulately striving for an ill-defined something that will transcend his middle-class life. Updike's satire never becomes so obvious as that of Lewis, though.

Mortality and what lies beyond greatly concern Updike in the Rabbit books. Whether seen in the accidental drowning in the first novel of Rabbit's infant daughter, overlooked in the bathtub by his drunken wife, or in his own death by heart attack in *Rabbit at Rest*, the novels are suffused by the nearness of death. This might be less remarkable a trait in the novels written later in Updike's life, but the preoccupation is present even in the first, published when the author was twenty-eight. Rabbit is implicated in his daughter's death, for he has abandoned his wife (running forms a major motif of the novel) and is not at home. Little Becky, less than a month old, dies on the first day of summer.

Also in view in these books is Updike's method as professional man of letters working assiduously to produce novel after novel. Not every one of his works is equally distinguished, but by opting to work steadily rather than only swinging for the fences, he produced more hits than misses. For the Rabbit books alone, he earned two Pulitzer Prizes, a National Book Award, and a National Book Critics Circle Award. The third novel, *Rabbit Is Rich,* was the most lauded.

Rabbit, Run

The first novel in the tetralogy, *Rabbit, Run,* introduces Harry and his wife, Janice, each in characteristic modes. Nicknamed "Rabbit" as a child partly for "a certain nervous flutter under his brief nose" (5), at age twenty-six Harry is seen getting into a pickup basketball game with neighborhood kids while walking home from his job demonstrating the MagiPeel kitchen gadget in five-and-ten stores. At six feet three inches and still a natural athlete, he obviously outclasses the kids. They are surly to have him intrude, but basketball is something he knows. Eight years before he had been a high school star; now he has become anonymous, an unknown "piece of the sky of adults" that hangs over the boys. Only the one who played on his side, another natural athlete, "continued to watch him with disinterested admiration after the others grew sullen" (7).

Past the substantial houses on the plain, Rabbit climbs to a hillside neighborhood of triple-deckers built in the 1930s, the place for those less successful. Mount Judge is a fictional counterpart to Updike's Shillington, Pennsylvania, boyhood home. (A small suburb of Reading, Shillington also appears fictionally as "Olinger" in some of his short stories.)

Janice, pregnant with their second child, is sitting and watching *The Mickey Mouse Club* on television with a cocktail in hand to blunt the pain of her varicose veins as Rabbit arrives in their walk-up apartment. The drink is not her first, and she does not look well. "She is a small woman whose skin tends toward olive and looks tight, as if something inside is straining against her littleness. Just yesterday, it seems to him, she stopped being pretty. With the addition of two short wrinkles at the corners, her mouth has become greedy; and her hair has thinned, so he keeps thinking of her skull under it. These tiny advances into age have occurred imperceptibly, so it seems just possible that tomorrow they'll be gone and she'll be his girl again" (8). Mortality and the end of youth are established thematically here, as well as Rabbit's sometimes self-deluding optimism.

Janice tries to bum a cigarette, but Rabbit threw his pack into a garbage can on the way home in an effort to give up the habit, and this plus his not drinking is infuriating to her. Rabbit does not find Jimmy the head Mouseketeer's homily on finding one's place in God's creation particularly inspiring but rather appreciates Jimmy's facial expression, a combination of pinching his mouth together and winking, "getting the audience out front with you against some enemy behind, Walt Disney or the MagiPeel Peeler Company, admitting it's all a fraud but, what the hell, making it likable" (10). The expression is utilitarian, and Rabbit decides that he can use it while demonstrating peelers and that fraud is "the base of our economy" (11). Jimmy's passing reference to religion (a major Updike theme) makes both Rabbit and Janice nervous: "God's name makes them feel guilty" (10).

The parameters of these two characters' lives in this and the subsequent novels are already set here. They are ordinary, not well matched, and really not individual enough to break away from each other or from their conventional lives, even though the main narrative thrust of the first novel is Rabbit's attempt to run from Janice and adult responsibility, first in an all-night car drive south, then in his affair with a larger and more intelligent woman, Ruth Leonard, who bears him a daughter and figures in the series.

Janice is a mess, and Rabbit tells her so. They argue without heat, habitually, over her purchase of a red swimsuit that her pregnant body cannot currently fit into and about her leaving their two-and-a-half-year-old son, Nelson, with her mother and their Ford Falcon economy car with his. When Janice fails to get a joke about her housewife status making her the ideal consumer for the MagiPeel, Rabbit decides, "There seems no escaping it: she is dumb" (13), a judgment that he will repeat throughout the tetralogy. Still he remembers Janice as the girl he once had made love to in a friend's borrowed apartment. They both then had worked at the same downtown department store, Krolls, which will disappear from the cityscape in later novels, leaving only a vacant lot and its memory as the city's economy changes over the years, echoing the changes in most American cityscapes over the same period of time as Americans (including the Angstroms) moved to the suburbs.

The problem of whether first to pick up car or child sickens him with its intricacy, a measure of how difficult daily life can be for him. Rabbit has to retrieve both child and car; neither at first seems more important than the other in his view, and he ponders which order of retrieval would better. He thinks approvingly of how Nelson "walks like a trooper, with choppy stubborn steps" (14–15), an early positive view of this character that may also hint at difficulties to come with respect to the boy's stubbornness. Rabbit's mother's continuing disapproval of Janice complicates the choice, and when Janice asks him to pick up a pack of cigarettes in a tone that suggests all is forgiven after their argument, he "senses he is in a trap. It seems certain. He goes out" (15). Rabbit is in a trap set by his own choices and limitations, and for the next thirty years he will try to escape or to acclimate.

Relief from domestic disharmony comes once he is outside in a fine description of Rabbit's evening walk through Mount Judge as the town grows dark and cool. Such set-piece descriptions evoke time and place and also distance readers for a while from the tensions of characters' lives. Rabbit walks past Norway maples and telephone poles that evoke memories of his earlier life, when he "loved to climb [the poles] . . . to where you could hear the wires sing" (15). His walk leads him across the town, past a boarded-up old stone farmhouse "which once commanded half of the acreage the town is now built on" near the aging Sunshine Athletic Association building. "There was no sunshine in it," and Rabbit remembers that his old high school coach, Marty Tothero, lives there after having been ousted from the high school as a result of an unspecified scandal (16). (Thus Updike neatly slips in this first reference to a character who will soon become a major one in the novel and the first of several mentors who attempt to shape Rabbit's choices.)

The forest on the actual Mount Judge seen rising above its namesake town is a part of Rabbit's memories, which also include the fear he felt as a boy in the woods where old cellar excavations lurked, a fear that "trills like an alarm bell you cannot shut off" and sent him back onto the blacktop of the road that climbs to the Pinnacle Hotel and a view of Brewer. Here is introduced the first reference to Rabbit's running.

Rabbit comes to his parents' house to the accompaniment of childhood memories of the marital arguments of neighbors who lived close, "the kitchen windows not six feet apart," then disputes regarding grass-cutting with new neighbors when the first neighbors moved away, and then memories of quarrels between his parents themselves (19). Unseen by those inside, he looks into his parents' kitchen window to see a scene of domestic tranquility, and under the spell of memory he momentarily mistakes Nelson in a high chair for himself as a child. His mother is concentrated on making Nelson eat a spoonful of beans; his father is just home from work, his shirt ink-stained (he is a printer); and his nineteen-year-old sister, Miriam, is "dolled up in gold and jet for Friday night" and wearing too much makeup (20), suggesting some of the directions in which her character will be developed.

Still unseen by those in the kitchen, Rabbit leaves this domestic scene untouched and walks to his mother-in-law's house a few blocks over on Joseph Street. (The Springer house on Joseph Street is a continuing locale, almost another character, throughout the tetralogy.) He is pleased to discover that the key is in the ignition of his '55 Ford, and thus he will not have to deal with either of the Springers, whom he finds challenging: "The Springers like to push you around" (21) is his complaint about them, focusing on the Ford, which Rabbit bought used from Springer's used car lot, probably more car than he could really afford but attractively priced. The Springer living room lights flash on as he first stalls, then cranks the Ford into life, and Rabbit takes off, heading toward Philadelphia (which he hates as "dirtiest city in the world") and listening to music on the car radio as he drives. He hears "Without a Song," "Secret Love," and "Autumn Leaves" (23), all sentimental songs popular in the 1950s. He drives past his own parents' house and then far beyond, out of the city onto country roads in an entrancing narrative blend of description and continuing memory. After a while he stops for gas at a roadside store and discovers that he has driven forty miles to get sixteen miles in a straight line away from home. "His goal is the white sun of the south like a great big pillow in the sky" (27). Since he just got paid, he has seventy-some dollars in his pocket to pay for gas, burgers, apple pie, and a glass of milk. Before he knows it, he is in Maryland, accompanied by a medley of popular songs, advertisements, and news on the radio. It is the evening of the equinox, and the next day will be spring. Here as in other of Updike's novels, action begins on or near the turnings of the seasons, linking his characters to the rhythms of the nature world.

Before midnight he is having coffee in a little café and realizes that "he is unlike the other customers. . . . He wonders, Is it just these people I'm outside or is it all America?" (30–31). A half-hour later he is lost. Remembering the comment of the man who had filled his gas tank earlier in the evening—"Figure out where you're going before you go there" (34)—he turns north and toward home, Updike having led readers through a masterful evocation of the American landscape. As dawn begins to tinge the building fronts of Mount Judge with pink, Rabbit parks in front of the Sunshine Athletic Association, near where he began his journey. He settles down to sleep in the front seat of the Ford but finds himself nervous that he might miss Marty Tothero. Waiting, he remembers in detail the first time he saw shy Janice nude, in the bathroom weeks after their wedding, and then he sees Tothero "walking away down the alley . . . looking stranger than Rabbit had expected . . . like a big tired dwarf" (37). This characterization may subtly echo those of *The Centaur*, where Pennsylvania characters all doubled as mythological beings. Tothero proves to be a contradictory and confounding character, not the simple, reliable mentor and guide who might suit a character as limited as Rabbit.

Tothero is delighted to see Rabbit; he says that the boys he coached never seemed to return, but here is the most talented of them all. Rabbit tells Tothero that he has run away from Janice, whom he describes as an alcoholic and dumb, and the coach seems sympathetic to her. He remembers her as Janice Springer from high school and comments, "Harry, that's a harsh thing to say. Of any human soul." Still Tothero offers Rabbit what he has requested, a place to sleep, and also advice.

> "Now, Harry, I'll give you the place to sleep provided, provided, Harry, that when you wake up the two of us have a serious, a long and serious talk about this crisis in your marriage. I'll tell you this now, it's not so much you I'm worried about, I know you well enough to know you always land on your feet, Harry; it's not so much you as Janice. She doesn't have your coördination. Do you promise?"
>
> "Sure. Promise what?"
>
> "Promise, Harry, we'll thrash out a way between us to help her."
>
> "Yeah, but I don't think I can. I mean I'm not that interested in her. I was, but I'm not." (39)

They climb together to Tothero's lair in the club's attic, a place of "old pinochle tournament charts and pool tables and some lumber and metal barrels and broken chairs with cane bottoms and a roll of chicken wire and a rack of softball uniforms." Tothero has an unmade army cot and "a bureau cleverly made of six beer cases wired together" with his clothing neatly organized (40), but everything else a mess.

Tothero watches Rabbit undress and climb into the cot, and Rabbit worries about the implications of this seeming voyeurism but then realizes that "it takes Tothero back in time" to when he had watched members of his teams change clothes in locker rooms, and Rabbit relaxes. He goes to sleep to paradoxically innocent memories of a suburban brothel he went to when serving in the Army in Texas during the Korean War, the madam a welcoming mother type and the prostitute he hired a sympathetic and realistic person who provided exactly what he paid for, no more or less. As he drifts off to sleep, "the clangor of the body shop [beside the Sunshine Athletic Association] comes up softly. It reminds him he is hidden and safe. While he hides, men are busy nailing the world down, and toward the disembodied sounds his heart makes in darkness a motion of love" (42). He is at peace, a state to which he perpetually aspires.

Tothero wakes Rabbit after six o'clock in the late afternoon, announcing that they are going out to eat with his girlfriend and that he has also got a girl for Rabbit. His previous concerns for Janice's welfare seem forgotten. Tothero explains, "You and I are two of a kind. . . . We know what the score is we know—," but at this Tothero is balked, can only repeat himself (46). The reader soon comes to suspect that he may not know any more about the workings of the world and human psychology than does Rabbit. Rabbit had expected to talk about Janice, and Tothero promises to do so "the moment our social obligations are satisfied" (43), a promise that he will not keep.

Rabbit changes into one of Tothero's shirts, fresh from the laundry. Though they are dissimilar in terms of physical stature, they wear the same size, 15 × 33, which Tothero explains is because Rabbit's arms are short for his height, a detail that suggests something magical and shape-altering about the situation, something similar about the two men, or just Tothero's incompetence as guide to the world. Rabbit is introduced to Tothero's card-playing cronies as they leave: "old men, mostly, but not very old, so their misshapen bodies have a nasty vigor" (46), a description that echoes Tothero's dwarflike vitality. Once in the Ford, Rabbit begins to drive at Tothero's direction but then is mostly left to find his own way. Tothero has changed moods and now calls Janice a "little mutt" (a characterization that Rabbit echoes throughout the tetralogy).

Tothero claims that "real women are dropping out of trees." One of them is Ruth Leonard, whom he has invited along to serve as Rabbit's date. She is seen by Rabbit as "fat alongside Margaret [Tothero's date], but not *that* fat. Chunky, more. But tall, five eight or nine" (48). By this she perhaps is implied to be thus a better match for Rabbit than the diminutive Janice. (In fact Ruth is identified as weighing 147 pounds, which at either height would put her in the middle of the normal weight range for women.) The two continue to discuss weight and height: "Just big outside," Rabbit says in characterizing himself to her, perhaps suggesting his emotional or intellectual limitations, and Ruth answers, "That's me too" (49), though in fact she proves to be intelligent, if a little morally loose. She went with three of the members of her high school's basketball team, she reports.

"Three at once?"

"In a way."

"Well, they looked tired."

> She laughs again . . . though he feels ashamed of what he has said, she is
> so good-natured and maybe was pretty then. (49)

The two share memories of a past high school basketball game between their respective schools. They both graduated in 1951 and hold to the same "Class of '51" view of life, a fact that pleases Rabbit.) All four share a meal in a newly opened Chinese restaurant, so recently converted from another cuisine that "pink paintings of Paris are still on the wall" (50), and Rabbit and Tothero offer memories of the past.

Drinking, Tothero pontificates on coaching: "'The coach,' he says, 'the coach is concerned with developing the three tools we are given in life: the head, the body, and the heart'" (54). Whether Rabbit possesses tools beyond his body is an open question, one of the most significant ones of the tetralogy. The two men remember past basketball games, with an emphasis on the stranger ones, nonconference games that did not mean anything, and championship games in which their team was defeated, since its strength consisted mostly of Rabbit's exceptional skill and not in a balanced ensemble of players. Tothero notes that Rabbit never fouled, perhaps an admirable (if unrealistic) trait in a player, and another clue to an appealing aspect of his character. Only teammate Ronnie Harrison—a character throughout the tetralogy—came close to complementing Rabbit's skill on the court. Surprisingly Ruth seems to recognize Ronnie's name, though when Rabbit quizzes her about him (he knows Ronnie as a "notorious bedbug" and describes him as a "shortish guy with kinky hair" and a "little bitty limp"), she reverses herself immediately: "No, I don't know. . . . I don't think so" (56–57). Later in the novel it is revealed that Ronnie and Ruth indeed slept together, spending a weekend in Atlantic City, and the revelation propels Rabbit and Ruth into an ugly crisis in their relationship.

Reminiscences completed, Tothero and Margaret leave the restaurant on a note of argument with perhaps a sexual component after she slaps him. They also leave the unpaid check, which Rabbit picks up. Rabbit plans to go to a hotel rather than return to the Sunshine Athletic Association, but instead he ends up going home with Ruth, paying her fifteen dollars as a contribution to the rent of her apartment. It becomes obvious to Rabbit that she is a low-level prostitute of sorts, who does not quite admit her profession but has no occupation otherwise.

They walk to her apartment (on the symbolically named Summer Street), and Rabbit embraces her perhaps too lustily after they enter. Ruth slaps him and tells him to get out, but instead of leaving, he feels he must explain himself:

He kicks the door shut with a backward flip of his leg. "Don't," he says, "I had to hug you." He sees in the dark she is frightened; her big black shape has a pocket in it which his instinct feels like a tongue probing a pulled tooth. The air tells him he must be motionless; for no reason he wants to laugh. Her fear and his inner knowledge are so incongruous: he knows there is no harm in him.

"Hug," she says. "Kill felt more like it."

"I've been loving you so much all night," he says. "I had to get it out of my system." (66)

She accepts his explanation, and Updike's description of their lovemaking pushes the limits of what was acceptable at the time of the novel's publication in its attention to detail. Ruth goes into the bathroom to insert her diaphragm, but Rabbit objects: "If you're going to put a lot of gadgets in this, give me the fifteen back" (67). Ruth has her own objection, that he is ordering her around as if they were married, but a "transparent wave" of feeling moves over Rabbit, and he calls to her, "Yes; let's be." Down on his knees (almost as if proposing), he takes off her shoes, wonders why women wear high heels, and follows her into the bathroom to watch while she urinates "primly, her back straight and her chin tucked in" (68). The details are matter-of-fact, perhaps incongruously reminding Rabbit of his and Janice's trying to toilet-train their son.

Back in the bedroom, Rabbit undresses Ruth, calling this their wedding night and kissing her. He presses his teeth into her throat as if to bite her, and she notes the apparent sadomasochism of Margaret and Marty's sexual relationship. Ruth complains, "Damn men . . . either want to hurt somebody or be hurt," but Rabbit has something else in mind, something gentler and more innocent than what Ruth expected: "I don't, honest. Either one" (69), he says.

Rabbit wins her over with his attention and praise for her body. "Clothes just fall from a woman who wants to be stripped," he thinks in a famous line. He even washes her face of its "crust" of makeup and "makes love to her as he would to his wife," since after marriage "Janice needed coaxing" (73). In time both Ruth and Rabbit come as he pays attention to her and repeatedly calls her pretty.

"You were a beautiful piece," he says from the pillow listlessly, and touches her soft side. Her flesh still soaks in the act; it ebbs slower in her.

"I had forgotten," she says.

"Forgot what?"

"That I could have it too."

"What's it like?"

> "Oh. It's like falling through."
>
> "Where do you fall to?"
>
> "Nowhere. I can't talk about it."
>
> He kisses her lips; she's not to blame. She lazily accepts, then in an after-flurry of affection flutters her tongue against his chin.
>
> He loops his arm around her waist and composes himself against her body for sleep. (75)

This perfect moment does not last, of course. Ruth has to get up, "baggy in nakedness," and go to the bathroom, and Rabbit remembers his distaste for aspects of female bodily function. But something also has been built between the two of them: their encounter has the feel of real lovemaking.

Pushing the Limits with Regard to Sexuality and Other Issues

The publication of *Rabbit, Run* contributed to Updike's becoming a chronicler of American sexual behavior and specifically to his part in the opening up of sexual subject matter in American fiction. As Adam Begley reports in his 2014 biography of Updike, a later scene in the novel involving fellatio created controversy with his lifelong publisher, Knopf. Ruth Leonard at Rabbit's urging kneels and sucks him. Alfred Knopf prevailed upon Updike to cut a little from the description, already somewhat indirect (201–2). In fact, compared to much of the rest of the sexual description in *Rabbit, Run,* the act is underplayed, without the direct yet lyrical description that makes the treatment of sex in the novel so different from much that had preceded it in print.

Updike was in illustrious company in his overall treatment of sexuality and in the general area of opening up the literary canon to more frank and realistic treatment of human experience. Vladimir Nabokov had preceded Updike by a couple of years with the 1958 novel *Lolita,* which deals with pedophilia, and the Post Office's ban on the mailing of D. H. Lawrence's *Lady Chatterley's Lover* (1928) had been overturned in court in 1959, with an unexpurgated U.S. edition finally appearing in 1960. Henry Miller's previously banned and highly graphic *Tropic of Cancer* (1934) was published in the United States by Grove Press in 1961, with accompanying obscenity cases from coast to coast, and the U.S. Supreme Court finally approved the edition in 1964.

Updike explicitly addressed the subject of pushing the limits of literary decorum, particularly regarding sexuality, in a *Paris Review* interview in 1968: "About sex in general, by all means let's have it in fiction, as detailed as needs be, but real, real in its social and psychological connections. Let's take coitus out of the closet and off the altar and put it on the continuum of human behavior. There are episodes in Henry Miller that have their human resonance;

the sex in *Lolita,* behind the madman's cuteness, rings true; and I find the sex in D. H. Lawrence done from the woman's point of view convincing enough. In the microcosm of the individual consciousness, sexual events are huge but not all-eclipsing; let's try to give them their size."

The morning after their first night together, Rabbit and Ruth make love again, less satisfyingly, "and he wonders if she pretends. She says not; no, it was different but all right. Really all right" (78). Meanwhile across the street people are arriving for church—it is Palm Sunday—and this prompts a prayer from Rabbit and then a discussion of religion with Ruth. As she is not a believer, Rabbit's profession of faith "grates against her" (79), and they argue as he prepares to leave.

> "I like you enough," she says in a preoccupied voice, tugging the bedspread smooth.
> "Enough for what?"
> "Enough." (80)

Ruth tells Rabbit that she likes him partly because he is bigger than she (she complains that smaller women seem to steal most of the big men), and when he asks why else she likes him, she says, "'Cause you haven't given up. In your stupid way you're still fighting" (80). This is enough of a positive reaction from her that Rabbit proposes to go out to the grocery for something for Ruth to cook for their lunch. "'What do you like?' she asks. . . . *What do you like?* He has her. He knows he has her" (81). Rabbit now intends to stay.

After lunch he goes to his and Janice's apartment, picks up his clothes, and leaves behind his key and the Ford parked at the curb. On the way out, he encounters his pastor, the Episcopal reverend Jack Eccles. (The name suggests Eccles's role as a representative of the Christian Church, *ecclesia* in Latin.) Eccles, who is Rabbit's age or a little older, has been looking for him and offers him a ride in his Buick. He was called by Janice's mother in the middle of the night about Rabbit's disappearance, and now he is on Rabbit's case—"this, and a death yesterday" (92). In response to Eccles's questioning, Rabbit confesses that he has no plan of action and that he left Janice mainly because she asked him to buy cigarettes: "It's the truth. It just felt like the whole business was fetching and hauling, all the time trying to hold this mess together she was making all the time. I don't know. It seemed like I was glued in with a lot of busted toys and empty glasses and the television going and meals late or never and no way of getting out. Then all of a sudden it hit me how easy it was to get out, just walk out, and by damn it *was* easy" (91).

Eccles continues to challenge Rabbit's reasons for leaving, and asks why he thinks that the "muddle" of his life is different than that of any other young married man, why for any reason he might be considered exceptional. Rabbit has an answer, really one of the keys to the understanding of his character and of the direction of the entire tetralogy: "You don't really think there's any answer to that but there is. I once did something right. I played first-rate basketball. I really did. And after you're first-rate at something, no matter what, it kind of takes the kick out of being second-rate. And that little thing Janice and I had going, boy, it was second-rate" (92).

The statement is baldly straightforward, perhaps even shocking in its candor, but his striving for the irrecoverable and first-rate lost thing is what keeps Harry Angstrom fresh and optimistic as a character—and also poignant and even sometimes annoying as he remains mired in his second-rate adulthood. It also makes him the perfect vehicle for Updike's ongoing project, not yet fully realized in this first of the novels, of measuring American's rise and decline in parallel to the arc of Rabbit's life.

Just before the reverend drops him off near Ruth's apartment, Rabbit hears a rattle in the Buick's trunk that turns out to be made by a set of golf clubs, and Eccles invites him to play. "Rabbit knows he should run, but the thought of a game, and an idea that it's safest to see the hunter, make resistance" (94). The round is set for Tuesday. Eccles is "a listener by trade" in Rabbit's view (92), setting up a good deal of exposition of his motives. Their golf date also introduces Rabbit's interest in this most middle class of American males' sports, an interest that will grow and carry through the novels of the tetralogy.

Settling into a shared routine, Rabbit and Ruth next take a walk to the top of Mount Judge, something that he did repeatedly as a boy but that is new to her. She is awkward in her high heels (she has no other shoes) and then has to walk barefoot on the dirt path, so Rabbit takes off his shoes and socks to walk barefoot with her in what seems a gesture of empathy. At the top of the mountain, he thinks first of religion ("His day has been bothered by God: Ruth mocking, Eccles blinking—why did they teach you such things if no one believed them?"), and then he thinks of mortality ("Someone is dying. In this great stretch of brick someone is dying. The thought comes from nowhere: simple percentages" [98]). Religion and mortality become continuing thematic concerns of the tetralogy and, indeed, of much of Updike's work.

As he looks down at Brewer from the mountaintop cliff, Rabbit is frightened, wonders what he is doing there and why he is not at home. He begs Ruth to put her arm around him, she obliges, and he feels better, comforted, as they ride a bus back to the city instead of walking down the mountain (99). Again he has found solace and peace in this new relationship.

A few days later, another bus takes him to Rev. Eccles's house for their Tuesday golf date. In the meantime he and Ruth have been bowling and going to the movies, but he still has fourteen dollars left from his pay, and Ruth has five hundred dollars in a bank account. Eccles's wife, Lucy, greets him, looking younger at first than she is. When she turns to ascend the stairs to rouse the napping Eccles, Rabbit pats her on her firm bottom, giving in to an irresistible and characteristic impulse. There is enough disharmony in the Eccles household that she never bothers to tell her husband about the pat, despite being alone with him in the kitchen while Rabbit listens from the next room, waiting to hear her make the revelation. Rabbit and Eccles drive to the country club (where Rabbit once had caddied as a boy). They discuss Janice, who seems to be doing fine. Eccles has scouted out a job for Rabbit as gardener for one of his parishioners at forty dollars a week, so things are looking up, but their first hole of play is a nightmare of more strokes than Rabbit can count. Eccles plays like an old man yet still leads him. The stroke-by-stroke description of Rabbit's humiliation is drawn out, detailed, and harrowing, and in telling contrast to his own earlier description of his past excellence in basketball.

Then at the second tee, Rabbit swings too hard but still hits a perfect drive that rises into the air, carrying far beyond anything Eccles ever could manage. "'That's it!' he cries and, turning to Eccles with a grin of aggrandizement, repeats, 'That's it'" (116). Rabbit finds his moment of transcendent excellence and triumphs. Eccles remains a contrasting character, another young husband like Rabbit, but one who never has done anything excellent in spite of his role as clergyman and mentor.

As one might expect given the description of his timidity, Rabbit finds peace in the gardening job arranged by Eccles. He works in the garden of the wealthy, widowed Mrs. Smith throughout the summer while continuing to live with Ruth, play golf with Eccles, and ignore Janice and Nelson. Mrs. Smith has outlived her husband, the original gardener, and she loves to walk through the garden on Rabbit's arm—though she says that as a farmer's daughter she would have preferred that her husband had planted buckwheat rather than flowers, or so she had teased him while he was alive. A prize pink rhododendron is the garden's greatest specimen, unique in the United States and shipped from England before the Second World War at the then-exorbitant cost of two hundred dollars during the depths of the Depression. The Smiths brought it from New York City to Pennsylvania in the back seat of their Packard, a luxury car of the era that marks them as having been well-off.

In their conversations Mrs. Smith is pleased to discover that Rabbit shares her opinion of World War II. She identifies it rather than the Korean War as "the war"; Rabbit remembers collecting tin cans and buying war bonds and getting awards for doing so while in elementary school. During WWII Mrs.

Smith's officer son had been killed—in his late thirties—but still she feels that "it was a good war. It wasn't like the first. It was ours to win, and we won it. All wars are hateful things, but that one was satisfying to win" (120–21). This is an early hint of the tone of nostalgia that suffuses the tetralogy, probably a factor in its success with the reading public.

Mrs. Smith wonders if heaven would be like a garden and worries that such a heaven might not suit her, but Rabbit is blandly reassuring: "Well, maybe what looks like rhododendrons to her will look like alfalfa to you." And she is appreciative of his tact in her strenuous, upper-class way: "It's such a pleasure. . . . You and I, we think alike. Don't we. Now *don't we?*" (122). The tone of her statement measures their point of commonality but also shows the reader her privileged inability to see how different are their experiences of the world.

As spring draws to a close, Ruth and Rabbit go swimming at a public pool on Memorial Day, another step in the development of their relationship, and he experiences great pleasure in watching her body in a bathing suit: "The solid sight swelled his heart with pride, made him harden all over with a chill clench of ownership. His, she was his, he knew her as well as the water, like the water has been everywhere on her body" (123). This rings true of Rabbit's character and of the element of competition for domination that exists in his relationship with Ruth, perhaps his relationships with most women, but his attitude of possession leads his relationship with Ruth into a crisis. Updike's depiction of this possessiveness is one of the factors that lead feminist critics to question the value of his work, Ruth in fact proves to be one of a number of nuanced and sympathetic portrayals of women.

Consequences take up much of the center of the novel: not only the consequences of Rabbit's sexual urges, though these are clearly present, but also of his actions in general, something that Rabbit had been able to avoid during that Edenic summer. In his own view, he means well and is lovable. Updike depicts this in a short exchange as he and Ruth lie beside the pool:

"Oh, all the world loves you," Ruth says suddenly. "What I wonder is why?"

"I'm lovable," he says.

"I mean why the hell you. What's so special about you?"

"I'm a saint," he says. "I give people faith." Eccles has told him this. Once, with a laugh, probably meaning it sarcastically. . . . Rabbit took this to heart. He never would have thought of it himself. He doesn't think that much about what he gives other people. (124)

Rabbit says that he supports Ruth, though she now also has a job as a stenographer, and she asks him why he does not support his wife.

"Why should I? Her father's rolling in it."

"You're so smug, is what gets me. Don't you ever think you're going to have to pay a price?" (125)

The narration then slips easily into Ruth's point of view. She has been crying in the restroom at work and feeling sleepy and hungry (early signs of pregnancy, though not so identified directly by Updike or noticed as such by Rabbit), and she finds Rabbit mild, stupid, and "a menace," though "still he did have the mildness and was the first man she ever met who did" (125). Her thoughts turn (in a variation on Molly Bloom's soliloquy in the "Penelope" section from the ending of James Joyce's *Ulysses*) to what other men wanted, "some business their wives wouldn't give" (126), whether it be dirty words, whimpering submission, or fellatio. Memories of high school and her reputation there as a willing sexual partner have led her to the early knowledge that sex is "no mystery" (126) but something simple: "it must have been just the *idea* of [her]" (127, Updike's emphasis) that excited the boys she dated, not what they actually did with her. These experiences have made her wiser about men. Somehow Rabbit seems different, though, "beautiful for a man" and boyish, but maybe, she thinks (in a change of direction), not so different from other men, after all. Her thoughts are complicated or perhaps muddled; she is not a very deep thinker, but neither is she shallow like Janice, and she is worried by Rabbit's developing sense, somehow fostered by Eccles, that he is not "acting wrong, but now he's got the idea he's Jesus Christ out to save the world just by doing whatever comes into his head" (128). His "soft cocksure voice" and smugness infuriate her, bringing her to tears as her soliloquy ends. "'I'll tell you,' he says. 'When I ran from Janice I made an interesting discovery.' The tears bubble over her lids and the salty taste of pool-water is sealed into her mouth. 'If you have the guts to be yourself,' he says, 'other people'll pay your price'" (129). Ruth's soliloquy establishes her as a realistic, nuanced, and believable character, not the simple "hooer" that Rabbit sometimes has called her in moments of stupidity.

The novel next turns to Eccles for a change of pace delaying Rabbit's fall and for alternative points of view on Rabbit as the young and somewhat naive clergyman travels the city, trying to set things right according to his lights. His first visit is to the Springers' house to see Mrs. Springer. In the backyard Nelson is being slightly bullied over a couple of red plastic trucks by Billy Fosnacht, who becomes his lifelong friend. Mrs. Springer is watching the boys in Janice's absence but shows an "ability to create uneasiness" (129) that nonplusses Eccles and may be a partial explanation of why Rabbit ran. She complains about Eccles's golf dates with Rabbit, not understanding that he intends them as a part of his mission to get to know, understand, and perhaps convince Rabbit to return home. "He's a good man, for one thing," Eccles insists, but Mrs. Springer's response is "Good for what?" (130). She is not sympathetic to Eccles, and she responds negatively to Nelson's distress at the loss of the toys. "I don't know why the boy is such a sissy. . . . Or maybe I do. . . . He's like his dad: spoiled. He's been made too much of and thinks the world owes him what he wants" (132). Eccles's defense of Nelson as only wanting his own toy trucks segues into Mrs. Springer's immediate defense of Janice as without fault in the breakup, and it seems to Eccles that she blames him along with Rabbit for the current situation and does not believe, as he does, that Rabbit will return to his marriage.

Eccles's thankless rounds take him next to the Angstroms' home, where Rabbit's mother is sure that Janice is the one to blame for the muddled situation: "I never wanted him to go with the girl in the first place. Just to look at her you know she's two-thirds crazy" (137). She also blames Janice for her looking down on the Angstroms' run-down duplex and for her inability to look one in the eye. When Eccles defends Janice as shy, Mrs. Angstrom is scathing: "Shy! She wasn't too shy to get herself pregnant so poor Hassy [sic] has to marry her when he could hardly tuck his shirt-tail in" (138). When Mr. Angstrom comes home from his job at the printing plant (into which trade he wishes Rabbit had followed), he is sympathetic to Janice, and an argument explodes, with Eccles siding with Angstrom, as he always tends to side with the weaker party. Rabbit's sister, Mim, comes in also, dressed to go out on Friday evening, her apparel faintly foreshadowing the fact that she becomes a prostitute later in the tetralogy.

Having escaped the Angstroms, Eccles next travels to the Angstroms' aging pastor, German Lutheran Fritz Kruppenbach, who condemns the younger pastor's efforts as "the story of a minister of God selling his message for a few scraps of gossip and a few games of golf. . . . You say role. I say you don't know what your role is or you'd be home locked in prayer. *There* is your role: to make yourself an exemplar of faith. *There* is where comfort comes from: faith, not what little finagling a body can do here and there, stirring the bucket. . . . There is nothing but Christ for us. All the rest, all this decency and busyness, is nothing. It is Devil's work" (147). Kruppenbach is called away to his dinner, and after leaving the older pastor's house, Eccles sits depressed in his car, thinking in one moment that he has been "flagellated with an insane spiel" and then in the next moment, "He's right, he's right" (147).

Eccles knows he is wanted at home by his wife, but instead he drives to a drugstore, where he is greeted by the girl behind the counter, a member of his church's youth group, and he also meets two parishioners "buying medicine or contraceptives or Kleenex. It is here that in truth they come to find the antidotes to their lives. He feels at home; Eccles feels most at home in Godless public places" (148). The young pastor drinks a couple of glasses of water while waiting for the ice-cream soda he has ordered. He is at peace, and religion seems ironically irrelevant in his world.

The novel next moves back to Rabbit and Ruth, spending an evening in a nightclub in the "the south side of Brewer, the Italian-Negro-Polish side," which Rabbit distrusts as he distrusts all that seems unfamiliar to him. The somewhat seedy Club Castanet was named "during the war when the South American craze was on," but it reminds Rabbit of an undertaker's, "a fortress of death" where one can become embalmed by drink (148). Ruth's friend Margaret had phoned to suggest the excursion to the club, where Rabbit finds himself enthralled by the "soft purple shadows" on the bare back of the African American waitress as she takes their orders, walking to and fro (149). When Margaret arrives to join the party, she is no longer with Marty Tothero as she had been earlier but with Ronnie Harrison, who seems to have become intrusive, sexually insistent, and annoyingly successful. Ronnie mocks Tothero as a coach and indicts Rabbit as "not a team player"; he also reveals that he once spent a weekend in Atlantic City with Ruth (152). Tension between Rabbit and Ronnie is high, devolving into crude sexual jokes. When Mim shows up at another table with a date, Ronnie makes the suggestion that she is a tramp with whom he also has slept. This all makes Rabbit sore. He goes over and bullies Mim's date, half insults Ronnie, and tells Ruth to leave with him. Aggrieved that no one else seems to understand his reasons for anger, Rabbit argues with Ruth on the walk back to their apartment, throwing her past sexual experiences at her and particularly her experiences with Ronnie. This is the lead-up to the fellatio episode that sours their relationship. In Ruth's point of view, Rabbit stands naked "by the dull wall in his brilliant body," and as Ruth slides off her clothes, she feels cold, "her temperature being divided or something"—it is obvious again to the reader, though not to her or to Rabbit, that she is pregnant. (There are other hints of the pregnancy in the Club Castanet scene as well.) Her ambivalence in this scene is in marked contrast to her earlier love of Rabbit's physical beauty, and this suggests a change—not a good one—in the dynamics of the relationship.

The ensuing fall of Rabbit and Ruth's relationship from idyll into the past tense is rapid. That same night he gets a call from Eccles (whose own marriage is in no great state, particularly after he comes home late after spending time at the drugstore). Eccles is relaying a message left with his wife by Mrs. Springer: Janice is in labor. As Rabbit leaves for the hospital, he asks Ruth to talk to him, but she stays under the covers, ignoring him, "heavy and sullen and her body hidden" (164). He is guilty about the act he forced on her, "kept wanting to lift her up and hug her in simple thanks and say *Enough you're mine again* but some-how couldn't bring himself to have it stop and kept thinking the *next* moment until it was too late, done." Her stillness frightens him, and he poses an ultima-tum: "Ruth. Hey. If you don't say anything I'm not coming back. Ruth" (165).

Rabbit feels as if Ruth is dead under the covers, ominously like a draped body at an auto accident. He feels manipulated by her silence and then angry at what he perceives as manipulation, and he leaves. The novel stays in the room with Ruth, however, and her insecurities about her weight and her desire to have again what she had a moment before: Rabbit in the room with her, calling her "Sweet Ruth." As the scene ends, she leaves the bed and kneels before the toilet, unable to throw up but somehow pleased to be there, and it is obvious that she is pregnant: "in her faint state it comes to seem to her that this thing that's making her sick is some kind of friend" (166).

The scene between Rabbit and Ruth and its aftermath is a sad moment, maybe the saddest in the entire tetralogy: these two limited but also very human and vulnerable characters lose a connection that makes them more than they otherwise are when with other characters or apart. In the subsequent books, Updike brings the two of them close to each other again and again in one way or another, perhaps more often in Rabbit's imagination than in physical reality. Rabbit is drawn to Ruth repeatedly, and repeatedly he runs away from her.

Updike's choice to move Rabbit and Ruth apart is sound in a narrative sense. It is a measure of the strength of his characterization that the separa-tion should simultaneously be so regrettable to a reader and so apt in helping to convey the author's view of America as a lost paradise whose inhabitants are ever seeking to recover something from its mythic past. (A parallel to *The Great Gatsby* can be inferred. If F. Scott Fitzgerald's Jay Gatsby is a potentially extraordinary man losing his direction in the changing America of the early 1920s, Harry Angstrom is an ordinary man with only one extraordinary talent, basketball, losing himself in the late 1950s and in the decades that followed.)

Rabbit's fall is rapid and prosaic and seems little resisted by him. In one moment he is with Ruth; in the next he is at the hospital and pulled back into his relationship with Janice, a woman about whom there is nothing transcen-dent, larger than life, or even appealing beyond the trim figure that she manages to regain after their daughter's birth and maintains into late middle age. Rabbit focuses on that one feature of her, to the exclusion of anything more worthy or lasting. In another of the many ironies surrounding Rabbit's abandonment of Ruth, Eccles tells Rabbit, "I'm very proud of you" regarding his return to Janice (164), and in the Catholic hospital's waiting room, he offers Rabbit a cigarette that seems like "a wafer of repentance" (168). Rabbit worries that as a conse-quence of his sin—"a conglomerate of flight, cruelty, obscenity and conceit;

a black clot embodied in the entrails of the birth" (169)—either Janice or the baby will die. His mood is not helped by the arrival of Janice's parents; while Mr. Springer says a modest hello, Janice's mother is hostile, suggesting Rabbit go "back to where you've been living because she's doing just fine without you and has been all along" (172).

In the course of things, the obstetrician arrives in the waiting room, congratulates Rabbit on "a beautiful little daughter . . . a normal delivery" (172–73), and asks his permission to let Mrs. Springer go in to see Janice. Mrs. Springer apparently has been harassing the staff, and they will be glad to do what it takes to make her go away. Rabbit, surprised to find himself in a position of authority, allows her to see Janice first, but once he is admitted to the hospital room, he discovers that Janice wanted to see not her mother but him. She tells him that Nelson has been asking when he will come home. "'Oh, damn,' he says, and his own tears, that it seemed didn't exist, sting the bridge of his nose. 'I can't believe it was me, I don't know why I left'" (176). Janice wants kisses from him and proposes bedtime conversation and lovemaking, despite the anesthetic that still numbs her from the waist down.

In the aftermath of his encounter with Janice, and prompted by Eccles, Rabbit does not go back to Ruth or even to his parents' house and instead spends the night in Eccles's spare room. There he "draws backward into sleep like a turtle drawing into its shell. Sleep this night is not a dark haunted domain the mind must consciously set itself to invade, but a cave inside himself, into which he shrinks while the claws of the bear rattle like rain outside" (177). Rabbit is truly caught, by his fears, his conventionality, and his inability to assert himself in any positive sense.

He wakes after noon the next day and eats a bowl of Cheerios in the kitchen while Lucy Eccles reveals that her husband has described him to his children as "the naughty man who's going to stop being naughty" (179). When she asks if he is "born anew" (180), Rabbit says that he feels about the same, that "last night driving home I got this feeling of a straight road ahead of me; before that I was sort of in the bushes and it didn't matter which way I went," and then, on a solipsistic tangent, "He thinks, *She wants me*" of Lucy (180). Whether this represents a realistic appraisal or merely his ego at work is not entirely clear; in any case, caught in transition between two other women, it is hardly to his credit. He thinks of Janice, which "perhaps seals shut something in his face," and Lucy turns away.

The religious cast of Lucy's question seems lost to him, and his egocentric point of view rules, but she then challenges him again just before he walks out the door on the way to the hospital and Janice: "When his eyes reach Lucy's an amazing thing enters the silence. The woman winks. Quick as light: maybe he imagined it. He turns the knob and retreats down the sunny walk with a murmur in his chest as if a string in there had snapped" (182).

At the hospital Marty Tothero's wife appears to tell him that Tothero is an inpatient also, now immobilized by two strokes. Rabbit's mentor has become something else, and he has lost his potential guidance. When they meet, Tothero laboriously rotates his hand at Rabbit's touch and holds hands with his former pupil as Rabbit thanks him for his role in bringing him back to Janice: "You were very kind," he says, and in the silence as it seems as if Tothero also will speak (though as it turns out he cannot). Rabbit feels that "a certain force flows forth, a human soul emits its invisible and scentless rays with urgency" (184). Then Tothero's focus on Rabbit fades, and he moves to Janice's room, where she already is complaining of the pain of her stitches and seeming to find his expressions of repentance boring. Soon they are arguing about their apartment and Janice's ignoring the rent, and then they watch a television program that is recognizably *Queen for a Day,* in which three hapless women told of their life's disasters to a sympathetic host, competing to see which will win out over the other two by the depths of her suffering as measured by an audience applause meter, have her wishes granted, and become "queen for a day." Watching this program somehow soothes Rabbit, though before its denouement he is called by a nurse to see his newborn daughter. Despite his continued wondering about what happened in the aftermath of an auto accident in which the son of one of the potential queens lost an arm, the baby charms him. "The folds around the nostril, worked out on such a small scale, seem miraculously precise; the tiny stitchless seam of the closed eyelid runs diagonally a great length, as if the eye, when it is opened, will be huge. In the suggestion of pressure behind the tranquil lid and in the tilt of the protruding upper lip he reads a delightful hint of disdain. She knows she's good. What he never expected, he can feel she's feminine, feels something both delicate and enduring in the arc of the long pink cranium, furred in bands with black licked swatches" (187). Later in the tetralogy, at the conclusion of *Rabbit Is Rich,* Rabbit holds his granddaughter, and the description (and his wondering reaction) will be remarkably similar and similarly wonderful.

Janice and Rabbit name the baby Rebecca June: Rebecca because it is Janice's mother's first name and June because the baby was born in June, Rabbit knows no other Junes, and it shares the initial letter of Janice's name. He and Janice seemingly will settle quickly back into domesticity. Janice's father has been keeping up the rent on their apartment without telling Janice, and Rabbit and Nelson move back into it while awaiting Janice's release from the hospital. Nelson is almost three and able to be helpful. Rabbit looks out the apartment window and "thinks, *My valley, My home.*" He settles into the apartment;

"every crevice, every irregularity in the paint clicks against a nick already in his brain" (189). As usual the familiar is comforting to him.

Settling up, Rabbit goes to quit his gardening job with Mrs. Smith. (His father-in-law now has set aside a sales job for him on one of the car lots.) "It was sort of like Heaven" (191), Rabbit tells her of the garden, and she replies that keeping her late husband's rhododendrons alive has been a sort of a "religious duty" to her. She thinks that she will not be there to see the flowers bloom the next year:

> "You kept me alive, Harry; it's the truth; you did. All winter I was fighting the grave and then in April I looked out the window and here was this tall young man burning my old stalks and I knew life hadn't left me. That's what you have, Harry: life. It's a strange gift and I don't know how we're supposed to use it but I know it's the only gift we get and it's a good one." Her crystal eyes have filmed with a liquid thicker than tears and she grabs his arms above his elbows with hard brown claws. "Fine strong young man," she murmurs, and her eyes come back into focus as she adds, "You have a proud son; take care." (192)

He feels as a blessing her final "Goodbye, I wish you well. I wish you well" (193).

In the next week, he takes Nelson to softball games played by boys wearing the uniform of the Sunshine Athletic Club but feels that he has moved beyond their world of competition and striving. Having given nature its ransom, children, it "is through with us and we become, first inside, and then outside, junk. Flower stalks" (194) like the ones he had burned in Mrs. Smith's garden.

He finds visits to his Springer in-laws now pleasing but a single visit with his own mother uncomfortable. She is angry and concerned about what will happen to Ruth. When Rabbit's father suggests Nelson will become an athlete, she retorts that he will not because "he has those little Springer hands" (196). Mim is not much present any more, and Rabbit notes how shabby their house is compared to the Springers'.

Alone in the apartment with Nelson, Rabbit is contented until the child goes to sleep, and then he fears that Nelson's sleep will become "so heavy . . . it might break the membrane of life and fall through to oblivion" (197). His thoughts of mortality alternate with memories of his past life, including his time with Ruth, and with masturbation. Still there is a sort of peace and security to his days alone there with Nelson before Janice comes home.

A crucial scene in the novel is the death of the infant Becky as a drunken Janice attempts to give her a bath in an adult-sized bathtub and somehow loses her beneath the soapy surface of the water. The incident introduces a motif of loss and desire for a daughter that carries forward through subsequent novels, often linked with water and the risk of drowning—and with a sense of Rabbit himself adrift. It is preceded by a passage from Janice's point of view in which she becomes progressively drunker, blaming Rabbit for having left her in the night (much as he left Ruth) because of a miscommunication regarding sex. Home from the hospital and still with stitches from her episiotomy, she reacts positively to a loving massage but negatively when Rabbit's insistent sexual urges make her feel that he treats her more like a convenience than a partner. He rushes out much in the same way that he earlier had left Ruth after their sexual encounter, and once he is gone, Janice is overwhelmed by caring for Nelson and Becky, drinks more and more, and causes the baby's death. Again, Janice is a mess, but Rabbit is also a mess, torn between his attraction to Ruth and to Janice, feeling more connected almost always to an imagined woman than to whichever woman is emotionally closer to him at the moment. After leaving Janice he tries to go back to Ruth, but she is not home, so he spends the night in a cheap hotel and avoids going to work at the Springers' used car lots for several days. Mr. Springer has been more than understanding even by Rabbit's self-serving lights.

Becky's funeral is the first of several in the novels, another continuing concern as Updike explores the meaning of death to his characters and also the somewhat ambiguous meanings of religion. A major strand in criticism of his works takes off from his religious concerns, and Updike returns to religion both seriously and satirically throughout his career.

After the funeral Rabbit takes a characteristic misstep. Guilty, he feels accused by the mourners and insists to them, "I didn't kill her."

This comes out of his mouth clearly, in tune with the simplicity he feels now in everything. Heads talking softly snap around at a voice so sudden and cruel.

They misunderstand. He just wants this straight. He explains to the heads, "You all keep acting as if I did it. I wasn't anywhere near. She's the one." He turns to [Janice], and her face, slack as if slapped, seems hopelessly removed from him. "Hey it's O.K.," he tells her. "You didn't mean to." He tries to take her hand but she snatches it back like from a trap and looks toward her parents, who step toward her.

His face burns. His embarrassment is savage. Forgiveness had been big in his heart and now's it's hate. He hates his wife's face. She doesn't see. She has a chance to join him in truth, and she turned away. He sees that among the heads even his own mother's is horrified, blank with shock, a wall against him; she asks him what have they done to him and then she does it too. A suffocating sense of injustice blinds him. He turns and runs.

Uphill exultantly. He dodges among the gravestones. Dandelions grow bright as butter among the graves. (252)

Rabbit runs away from the gravesite, climbing up toward Mount Judge (pursued by Reverend Eccles, whom he outdistances) and feeling lost and frightened in the woods, "the surrounding trees . . . too tall for him to see any sign, even a remote cleared landscape, of civilization" (255). He remembers the forest as a refuge when he was a child but feels that it now has turned threatening (forgetting that it had threatened him then also). He comes across a cellar hole as he flees, "ruined evidence of a human intrusion into a world of blind life" (256). Eventually he finds his way to a road, and he tries to call Eccles for advice, but Lucy Eccles hangs up the phone on him. He does eventually find Ruth at her apartment. She finally reveals she is pregnant with his child; she considered abortion but was unable to go through with it. He professes his love to the understandably skeptical Ruth, and she calls him "Mr. Death himself" for the death of Becky and of their love (262) but then says (sarcastically?) that she will take him back—if he divorces Janice. If not she will be dead to him, she says, and their baby will be, too. In the end, while walking around the block to collect himself, he looks to the window of the church opposite the apartment, but it is dark, unlit because of "church poverty or the late summer nights or carelessness." There is light in the streetlights about him, though, and he again runs from his muddled life: "with an effortless gathering out of a sweet panic growing lighter and quicker and quieter, he runs. Ah: runs. Runs" (264).

Rabbit Redux

Updike apparently had not conceived *Rabbit, Run* as the first book in a series. To an interviewer from the American Academy of Achievement, he explained the impulse behind the second novel, *Rabbit Redux,* in which the series really begins to gain traction in its exploration of distinctly American themes and subject matter:

> When I had run out of subjects, I thought . . . "Well, why not tell what happened and bring Rabbit back." This was during the late '60s, when there was a lot of turmoil in America, and so I brought him back this time as kind of an everyman who is witnessing the pageant of protest and disturbance, distress, drug use, everything, almost everything was in that book, including the moon shot. In fact, the moon shot is kind of a central event in it, so that

the Rabbit who came back the second time was a much more purposefully representative American than my initial Rabbit.

This second Rabbit novel begins at what should be a literal high point for the United States, on the day when the Apollo 11 NASA mission blasted off on its successful voyage to the moon. The conversation between Rabbit and his father in the Phoenix Bar after work ("with a girl nude but for cowboy boots in neon outside and cactuses painted on the dim walls inside" [4]), however, has to do not with that transcendent effort but with the decline of Rabbit's mother's health from Parkinson's disease, worries about what it might cost to put her in a nursing home, and rumors that Janice is having an affair, which much upset his mother despite Rabbit's denials. His father drinks Schlitz beer, a solid, working-class brand; Rabbit, improbably, drinks daiquiris. The rocket's liftoff is replayed again and again on the bar's television set, but "the men dark along the bar murmur among themselves. They have not been lifted, they are left here" (9) in an America where an honest day's work seems to have come to count for almost nothing, and the image's suggestion of phoenixlike rebirth through purifying fire seems distant and unlikely. A few days later Rabbit will be discussing with his father-in-law less uplifting news, Sen. Edward Kennedy's auto accident on Nantucket, in which Mary Jo Kopechne, a twenty-eight-year-old civil rights activist and secretary riding with him in the early morning hours after a party, was drowned, and the senator did not act with alacrity to rescue her, apparently for fear of scandal. (Like Rabbit and his creator, Kopechne was a native of Pennsylvania.) Also, though less emphasized by Updike, race riots are taking place.

While beautifully written, *Rabbit Redux* is also the ugliest and most violent book of the tetralogy. It reflects the uncertainty of the time, particularly for those men such as Rabbit and his father left behind in bars in fading industrial cities such as Brewer and facing women with new, nontraditional concerns and desires, and children who do not appreciate their lives and personal sacrifices.

Rabbit and the Postindustrial Economy: The Linotype

Early in *Rabbit Redux* the reader learns that Rabbit now is working with his father, Earl, at Verity Press, both as Linotype operators. This is a significant job for Updike, his character, and the state of American intellectual life, as the Linotype machine, introduced in 1886, made possible rapid composition of type for newspapers and books and thus greater communication throughout the United States. Previously type had been set by hand, a bottleneck in the printing process since fast steam and later electrically powered presses had existed since the 1830s. Otto Mergenthaler, a German immigrant to the United

States, developed this practical typesetting machine, which had been a sort of Holy Grail for printers.

The Linotype was a wonderful, Rube Goldberg–like product of industrial engineering. All its functions were mechanically accomplished. It incorporated a keyboard with separate keys for upper- and lowercase type, interchangeable magazines of various size and style type molds that sat atop the machine, and a mechanized system that assembled the molds into lines via a gravity feed and that evenly spaced the type forms for casting. After casting in lead the line of type (thus the name *Linotype*), it then resorted the molds for individual bits of type, returning them to the magazine via a conveyer belt powered by an electric motor. Simultaneously a pot of molten lead provided the raw material for casting the lines of type.

Watching or operating the machine, which measures roughly seven feet high and weighs at least a ton, with the operator usually sitting at a swivel chair before the keyboard, provides an immersive experience of clanging, clinking sound; heat; and the scorched smells of the melting lead. Linotype operators generally became excellent proofreaders—always having to check each newly cast line for errors and sometimes correcting copy on their own hook—and sometimes very well-informed men, since they spent their work days reading. (They were uniformly men, by the way.)

Verity Press does not connect Rabbit very well to the larger world, however. The press is holding on in the face of progress by printing tickets, posters, and the weekly *Brewer Vat,* "which specializes in city scandal since the two dailies handle all the hard local and syndicated national news." A German-language paper, the *Rocking-Chair,* dating back to the 1830s and previously printed by Verity, was allowed to lapse as its readers died out (24). When letterpress/Linotype production is replaced by Verity late in the novel (as happened generally in the United States in the 1970s and 1980s), it is a great loss for Rabbit. He loses his shared work connection to his father, and he loses a physically demanding occupation. His later work as a salesman, much like his early job demonstrating the MagiPeel in *Rabbit, Run,* does not really suit his strengths. He had tried out as a salesman at Springer Motors but moved to Verity Press instead in the time period between the two novels, for what he thought of as "honest work" (17).

Rabbit makes his way home from the bar by bus, headed to the new blue-collar suburb of Penn Villas (not to be confused with the more upscale Penn Park a little closer to the city), where twelve-year-old Nelson is waiting, though Janice is working late at Springer Motors. "The bus has too many Negroes" (10), he notes, who seem to be louder than they were during his boyhood. Rabbit thinks "educated tolerant thoughts" about them (by his own judgment) that are neither particularly educated nor particularly tolerant, though he has pretty much ceased to notice the race of the two black men working beside him at Verity Press. He feels "a certain fear; he doesn't see why they have to be so noisy" (11). Rabbit does appreciate the intelligence of Bill Cosby, a Philadelphia native then in the first flowering of his national fame as a standup comedian and television star. Black America's claim on the attention of white America will become a major focus of Rabbit Redux, reflecting the reality of the time, though that does not come until later sections of the novel.

Nelson is watching TV as his father arrives home. He hopes to get a new minibike like the one his friend Billy Fosnacht owns. Rabbit tells him the minibike is a sop to Billy from his divorcing parents and makes it clear that he will not be paying for one for Nelson or even assisting if the boy saves part of the cost himself. Throughout this first section of the novel and into the second, Nelson is hugely needy, an ignored child, though not yet the annoying, clueless, and self-destructive young man that he becomes in the later books. He achingly wants the minibike, as well as a hi-fi set like Billy's, a trip to a minor-league baseball game (the Brewer Blasts) with Rabbit and Grandpa Springer, who will pay for the tickets, and particularly to see director Stanley Kubrick's *2001: A Space Odyssey* during a planned evening out with his mother and father that instead turns out to center on his father's impassioned but ill-considered defense of the war in Vietnam—and Rabbit's growing realization that Janice actually is having an affair. Their family dinner at a Greek restaurant before the movie is an exercise in uneasiness caused by the unfamiliar menu and compounded by the arrival of Greek American Springer Motors salesman Charlie Stavros, Janice's lover, with whom she previously has dined at this establishment. Nelson ends the dinner in a panic that they will miss the beginning of the movie—the famous sequence in which a prehistoric human ancestor tosses a bone tool into the air and it becomes an orbiting space station, suggesting the evolutionary link of ape to *Homo sapiens*—though the decidedly unperceptive Charlie reassures him that the scene is nothing to get excited about. Eventually mother, father, and child sit close to the screen (having arrived at the last minute, with Janice slipping in late after spending a few extra moments with Charlie), overwhelmed by Kubrick's images of their supposed near future. In this whole sequence of scenes, Rabbit's child is at his most appealing, vulnerable, and sympathetic—a far cry from Nelson as depicted in the next two novels.

When Janice finally had come home on the earlier evening, she slipped into bed beside Rabbit and felt "alive, jazzed up, and wants to talk, apologetic, wanting to make it up" for not coming home earlier. She makes a sexual advance, but he brushes it away, and when she then turns away from him, "he accepts this rejection." Rabbit has no sense that he first has rejected her, wonders if he should have given her a child to replace dead Becky. "Maybe that was the mistake. It had all seemed like a pit to him then, her womb and the grave, sex and death, he had fled her cunt like a tiger's mouth" (23). As elsewhere in Updike, death seems ever-present. With Rabbit Angstrom, fear is a near-constant companion as well.

In the later Greek restaurant scene with Janice, Nelson, and Stavros, Rabbit's fear of the changing world helps to propel his defense of U.S. involvement in Vietnam, but his sensitivity to the world around him does so as well. While he does not yet know that Stavros is Janice's lover, he seems to intuit it, and that feeds into his vehemence, but he is unable to say to Charlie what he really thinks: "Wherever America is, there is freedom, and wherever America is not, madness rules with chains and darkness strangles millions" (41). Updike supplies the words, unspoken by Rabbit; Rabbit is not articulate enough to express them himself, nor is he articulate enough really to speak to his wife about their marriage difficulties.

Over time Rabbit has come to frighten Janice, and ominously, "Harry likes this sensation" (31). Things have continued to deteriorate between the two, and there persists an undertone of annoyance to their interactions, part of the violent subtext of the novel, as when "she comes home . . . tucking the Falcon into the garage in that infuriating way of hers, just not quite far enough to close the door on the bumper" (52). She makes fun of him for being outside cutting the grass when she arrives, and she lies to him ("Women like to lie, Harry, it makes things more fun" [53]), including about sleeping with Charlie. When it becomes clear that she is doing so, things turn violent.

> "You dumb bitch," he says. He hits her not in the face but on the shoulder, like a man trying to knock open a stuck door.
> She hits him back, clumsily, on the side of the neck, as high as she can reach. Harry feels a flash of pleasure: sunlight in a tunnel. He hits her three, four, five times, unable to stop, boring his way to that sunlight, not as hard as he can hit, but hard enough for her to whimper; she doubles over. . . . Her sobbing arises muffled and, astonished by a beauty in her abasement, by a face that shines through her reduction to this craven faceless posture, he pauses. Janice senses that he will not hit her anymore. She abandons her huddle, flops over to her side and lets herself cry out loud—high-pitched, a startled noise. . . . Flecked with her own spit Janice cries, "I do, I do sleep with Charlie!"
> "Ah, shit," Rabbit says softly, "of course you do," and bows his head into her chest, to protect himself from her scratching, while he half-pummels her sides, half tries to embrace her and lift her. (55)

Scenes like this are the sort that have led feminists to criticize Updike, but the fight rings true, suggesting the depths of their simultaneous connection and estrangement. They confess to each other, Janice expressing the pleasure of her relationship with Stavros and Rabbit saying more about his past affair with Ruth Leonard, including that he had a chance encounter with her recently at Krolls department store. Ruth, now grown heavier, "pretty much blended in with those other fat bag-huggers you see downtown, but at the same time, still, it was *her*" (58). The two then have sex and Rabbit, in a reflection of his ambivalence about human connections, sexuality, and family ties, grants her permission to continue the affair—which she does, even leaving home to live with Stavros.

The first section of the novel ends with Rabbit and Nelson's much delayed visit to Rabbit's father and ill mother on the occasion of her birthday, also the day of the Apollo 11 moon landing. Janice already is living with Charlie at this point and so does not join them, and in any case she and Rabbit's mother still do not get along. Earl Angstrom is enthusiastic about the landing, relaying mission progress from the sewing room where the television resides, but no one else seems to feel the excitement. Says Earl, "We're on the moon, boys and girls! Uncle Sam is on the moon!" (81).

Tired and sick, Mary Angstrom gasps a comment appropriate to her condition and to the ambiguities of the novel's point of view on the United States in 1969: "That's just. The place for him" (81). The relayed messages between lunar orbiter and lander are mostly garbled as the Angstroms listen to them, and the television video feed is a matter of glaring shapes and shadows, difficult to interpret. Even astronaut Neil Armstrong's famous words on the occasion are heard with "a crackle [that] keeps Rabbit from understanding. . . . Rabbit's mother's hand with difficulty reaches out, touches the back of his skull, stays there, awkwardly tries to massage his scalp, to ease away thoughts of the trouble she knows he is in. 'I don't know, Mom,' he abruptly admits. 'I know it's happened, but I don't feel it yet'" (86).

He does feel it—or at least has the opportunity to do so—as the novel progresses. In a masterfully written and engrossing sequence of scenes, Rabbit meets the major characters Hubert "Skeeter" Farnsworth, young black Vietnam veteran, and Jill Pendleton, an eighteen-year-old runaway from an affluent Connecticut family, while at Jimbo's Friendly Lounge at the invitation of a black coworker, Buchanan (apparently named after the president). These seemingly fortuitous encounters have the effect of expanding the novel's exploration of late 1960s themes.

Rabbit has been separated from Janice for three or so weeks at this point in the novel, and Buchanan seems to take pity on him, inviting him to the bar

with great tact while simultaneously expressing his envy of Rabbit's close relationship with his father. He insists that he might be able to help with what he
assumes is bothering Rabbit: "You should be havin' your tail is all. You're a big
fellow" (88).

Rabbit encounters three women to deal with his libido, such as it is. On his
way to Jimbo's, he drops off Nelson for a sleepover with Billy Fosnacht. Billy's
separated mother, Peggy, with her walleye and doughy legs, is there, quite willing, it seems, to enter into a romantic relationship with Rabbit. While Billy and
Nelson leave her apartment to play in the parking lot with Billy's minibike,
Peggy and Rabbit share a drink and size each other up.

She praises Rabbit as a family man (something he has not quite thought of
himself as before), and for his forgiving nature toward Janice. "Well, I don't
know if I did such a great job with Janice. She has to live too," he says, and
then falls into a reverie, imagining Peggy's body beneath her clothes as he sits in
a leather armchair that might otherwise afford him a view of Brewer from her
eight-story apartment building. The two discuss ideas and even God in vague
terms, Peggy asking, "Don't you think God is people?" and Rabbit replying,
"No, I think God is everything that isn't people. I guess I think that. I don't
think enough to know what I think" (94). Peggy's response is "'Oh, you think
with'—and to assist her awkward thought she draws his shape in the air with
two hands, having freed them for this gesture—'your whole person.'" Having
exhausted theology, "she looks so helpless and vague there seems nothing for
Harry to do but step into the outlines of himself she has drawn and kiss her"
(95).

Rabbit is saved from further temptation by the reappearance of Billy and
Nelson. The latter apparently has wrecked the minibike, though the exact details of how it happened are unclear, and when Rabbit promises to pay for the
damage (and says that he will take Nelson home), the two boys "set up a wail-
ing for Nelson to spend the night"—friendship trumps injury for them. Rabbit
makes his escape, though Peggy makes her position clear: "Harry. . . . I'm usually here. If—you know" (96). Later in the novel, she is still available.

The time for his appointment with Buchanan is not yet near, so Rabbit
walks through West Brewer, wonderfully described in a fine set-piece as poised
between the old city remembered from the time of his boyhood—with people
sitting on porch steps in the city's original neighborhoods—and the new world,
in which Brewer is no longer the center of things. The direction to the future
is indicated by "virtual billboards in white on green—directing motorists to
superhighways" (97), the federal interstate system built after World War II that
bypassed and tended to make irrelevant the old city centers.

Rabbit stops along the way for a quick meal at Burger Bliss, killing time with the Lunar Special ("double cheeseburger with an American flag stuck into the bun") and a vanilla milkshake (97) before he ventures into Jimbo's Friendly Lounge, where all the other patrons are black. "Fear travels up and down his skin, but the music of the great green-and-mauve glowing jukebox called Moonmood slides on, and the liquid of laughter and tickled muttering resumes flowing; his entrance was merely a snag" (98). Buchanan greets Rabbit and deflects his order of a daiquiri: "Never. That is a lady's drink for salad luncheons" (98). It becomes clear that once out of the print shop and into his own milieu, Buchanan is a person of considerable wit and intelligence—and clear to the reader if not to Rabbit that he may have had something more than a casual purpose in mind with his invitation. He orders a stinger for Rabbit.

In a back booth, Buchanan introduces Rabbit to two people, a young man with "a little pussy of a goatee" who will become important in much of the rest of the book and an old and wrinkled woman smoking what Rabbit does not yet realize is a joint of marijuana.

> "This man," Buchanan is announcing, "is a co-worker of mine, he works right beside his daddy at Ver-i-ty Press, an expert Linotypist," giving syllables an odd ticking equality, a put-on or signal of some sort? "But not only that. He is an ath-e-lete of renown, a basketball player bar none, the Big O [Oscar Robertson, all-star National Basketball Association guard] of Brewer in his day."
>
> "Many years ago," Rabbit says, apologizing for his bulk, his bloated pallor, his dead frame. He sits down in the booth to hide. (99).

The old woman is Beatrice "Babe" Green, the second woman of the evening available to Rabbit, for a price. She makes her way in the world as best she can as a pianist and lounge singer—and perhaps also a seer of sorts. She takes Rabbit's hand and pronounces his fingers not so impressive but his thumb something else.

> "Do dig that thumb," she advises the air. She caresses his thumb's curve. Its thin-skinned veined ball. Its colorless moon nail. "That thumb means sweetness and light. It is an indicator of pleasure in Sagittarius and Leo." She gives one knuckle an affectionate pinch. (100)

> "This thumb here is extremely plausible. Under the right signs it would absolutely function. These knuckles here, they aren't so good. . . . But this here thumb," she goes back to caressing it, "is a real enough heartbreaker." (100)

Rabbit is hooked, his fear at Babe's alien nature overcome by her attention to him, her phallic interpretation of his thumb, and the fact that despite her age she is so well-kept: made up theatrically, dressed in "the blood-red color of a rooster's comb," with a throat that "drips jewels, a napkin of rhinestones or maybe real diamonds," and "a silver sequin pasted beside one eye. Accent the ugly until it becomes gorgeous" (99–100).

The young man, Skeeter, makes fun of Rabbit and his square whiteness (as he does in the rest of his appearances in the novel). Babe, however, is all consideration despite Rabbit's fear that the marijuana joint will hook him or that his drink will be drugged and he will end up as a fatality in Jimbo's of a color unexpected by the coroner.

Then Buchanan mentions the third woman. "Jill in tonight?" he asks (103), and Babe quite aptly prophesies, "That poor baby . . . just going to hurt herself and anybody standing near" (104). Rabbit guesses that Jill is white and an unwanted influence. (Buchanan later says as much, that her presence in Jimbo's and living with Babe brings unwanted attention from the authorities.) As Rabbit declares his intention of leaving, Buchanan urges him to stay, and Rabbit asks Babe to play for him. Her set at the piano is seen in another of Updike's set-pieces of evocative description harking back to an older, vanishing America:

What does Babe play? All the good old ones. All show tunes. "Up a Lazy River," "You're the Top," "Thou Swell," "Summertime," you know. There are hundreds, thousands. Men from Indiana wrote them in Manhattan. They flow into each other without edges, flowing under black bridges of chords thumped six, seven times, as if Babe is helping the piano to remember a word it won't say. Or spanking the silence. Or saying, Here I am, find me, find me. Her hands, all brown bone, hang on the keyboard hushed like gloves on a table; she gazes up through blue dust to get herself into focus, she lets her hands fall into another tune: "My Funny Valentine," "Smoke Gets in Your Eyes," "I Can't Get Started," starting to hum along with herself now, lyrics born in some distant smoke, decades when Americans moved within the American dream, laughing at it, starving on it, but living it, humming it, the national anthem everywhere. Wise guys and hicks, straw boaters and bib overalls, fast bucks, broken hearts, penthouses in the sky, shacks by the railroad tracks, ups and downs, rich and poor, trolley cars, and the latest news by radio. Rabbit had come in on the end of it, as the world shrank like an apple going bad and America was no longer the wisest hick town within a boat ride of Europe and Broadway forgot the tune, but here it all still was, in the music Babe played, the little stairways she climbed

and came tap-dancing down, twinkling in black, and there is no other music, not really, though Babe works in some Beatles songs, "Yesterday" and
"Hey Jude," doing it rinky-tink, her own style of ice to rattle in the glass.
As Babe plays she takes on swaying and leaning backwards; at her arms'
ends the standards go root back into ragtime. Rabbit sees circus tents and
fireworks and farmers' wagons and an empty sandy river running so slow
the sole motion is catfish sleeping beneath the golden skin. (106)

Skeeter offers Babe to Rabbit, fifty dollars for all night, "all ways you can
think up," but "sunk in her music, Rabbit is lost. He shakes his head and says,
'She's too good.'" The passage goes on another page, illustrating Updike's
descriptive power to evoke situation, mood, and nostalgia through this excursion into the classic American songbook, both the nostalgia of Rabbit in the
moment in Jimbo's and a nostalgia for a lost American Eden that many of
Updike's readers likely felt in 1970. Rabbit is overjoyed by the performance: "he
brims with joy . . . wants to shout love . . . to the sullen brother in goatee and
glasses" (107).

Then Jill arrives, "a small white girl . . . standing there prim, in a white dress
casual and dirty as smoke" (107). She helps to propel much of the action of
the rest of the novel, as Rabbit takes her home and sleeps with her, then finds
Skeeter moving in as well to provide him a primer on Black Power, history, and
the sociopolitical grievances of the late 1960s. And to provide object lessons in
the dynamics of power and oppression.

Rabbit perhaps would have been better off with Babe and nostalgia or even
with Peggy and the ordinary. Buchanan provides the introduction, passing off
to Rabbit the problem that is Jill.

> "Jilly's a poor soul," Babe volunteers, stirring within her buzz. "She's fallen
> on evil ways." And she pats Rabbit's hand as if to say, *Don't you fall upon
> these ways*. [Updike's emphasis.] (109)

> He is beginning to get the drift. They are presenting him with this prob-
> lem. He is the consultant honky. (110)

> He is Penn Villas, she is Penn Park. Rich kids make all the trouble. (110)

From the reader's standpoint, Jill provides necessary impetus to the story line.
At least in the short run, she also is a plus for Rabbit and Nelson. In the second
of the book's four sections, she goes home with Rabbit from Jimbo's and sleeps
with him, and when Nelson comes home from his own sleepover at quarter to
ten the next morning, despite his father's best efforts at concealment, he is surprised to discover an unexpected presence in his father's bed: "Dad, something

moved in your bed. . . . Aren't you going to call the police?" Rabbit suggests
that since it is a Sunday, the poor old police should be allowed to rest. Jill comes
downstairs, wrapped in a sheet, and proves quite able to deal effectively with a
startled twelve-year-old: "I'm Jill, you're Nelson. Your father told me all about
you."

> She advances toward him in her sheet like a little Roman senator, her hair
> tucked under behind, her forehead shining. Nelson stands his ground. Rab-
> bit is struck to see that they are nearly the same height. "Hi," the kid says.
> "He did?"
>
> "Oh, yes," Jill goes on, showing her class, becoming no doubt her own
> mother, a woman pouring out polite talk in an unfamiliar home, flattering
> vases, curtains. "You are very much on his mind. You're very fortunate, to
> have such a loving father."
>
> The kid looks over with parted lips. Christmas morning. He doesn't
> know what it is, but he wants to like it, before it's unwrapped. (129–30)

Jill soon moves into the Angstrom household, prompting harassing calls
from Janice to Rabbit that interrupt him at work (causing complaints from
Rabbit's boss) but on the whole proving a force for sanity despite her topless
sunbathing that prompts complaints from the neighbors and despite her occasional neurosis—and Rabbit's own ambivalence about allowing her in, as well
as about allowing her to reshape his self-centered sexuality to something more
appropriate to her needs. The strain of violence present in the novel shows
itself from time to time in his anger and bullying and even physical abuse of
her, and eventually her Porsche is parked annoyingly partway into the garage,
much as Janice earlier had parked the Angstroms' Ford Falcon. Jill's expensive
convertible is dirty and dented on one fender, but she is teaching Nelson to
drive in it, and Rabbit would be riding the bus all the time without it. A typical
late 1960s runaway from an upper-middle-class home and then from a lifeguard
boyfriend who tried to turn her on to heroin, Jill introduces Rabbit and Nelson
to the pleasures of actual cooking and wine by the half-gallon jug (Updike's satirical streak is never far from the surface) and invites herself and Rabbit along
on an all-day excursion by boat conducted by Billy Fosnacht's father.

In Janice's calls to Rabbit at work, she indicates that she is not pleased at
any of this: "I want that girl out of my home. I don't want Nelson exposed to
this sort of thing," She says, to which Rabbit replies, "What sort of thing? You
mean the you and Stavros sort of thing?" alluding to the fact that Nelson has
been regularly visiting the two of them in Stavros's apartment (133).

"Come back to the house, I'm sure she'll go."

Now Janice thinks. Finally she states: "If I come back to the house, it'll be to take Nelson away."

"Try it," he says, and hangs up. (134)

He supposes Stavros can get her legal advice. But, far from feeling Stavros as one of the enemy camp, he counts on him to keep this madwoman, his wife, under control. Through her body, they have become brothers. (135)

This brotherhood bond continues into the future, as in subsequent novels Rabbit and Stavros continue an amicable relationship and eventually work together at Springer Motors right up to the point of Stavros's death caused by the weak heart that already is a factor in *Rabbit Redux,* providing a convenient excuse for his eventual dumping of Janice.

Jill offers Rabbit contentment, but there are continued worries, particularly regarding the state of Rabbit's marriage and how it will impact his relationship with the young woman. Stavros is sure that he cannot marry Janice—he seeks Rabbit out in the Phoenix Bar after work one day and admits as much: "Her staying on with me gives her expectations we can't fulfill. Marriage isn't my thing, sorry. With anybody. . . . She wants what every normal chick wants. To be Helen of Troy. There've been hours when I gave her some of that. I can't keep giving it to her. It doesn't hold up." Stavros asks if Rabbit will take Janice back, and Rabbit coldheartedly suggests, "Kick her out and see. She can always go live with her parents" (155). Stavros wishes to avoid stress from Janice, particularly given the parlous state of his heart, and Rabbit tells him that everything in his relationship with Janice is just like Rabbit's own relationship with her used to be, underlining their sense of brotherhood or of mutual responsibility for her.

Stavros is not the only one who wants something from Rabbit. Buchanan edges up one day in late summer at work, comments on how well the relationship with Jill seems to be working out, and puts the hit on Rabbit for twenty bucks to ease the back-to-school bite of his "oh . . . say five, that's been counted" kids (159). Rabbit calls it a loan, but he thinks he knows better. The bill for his summer of pleasure with Jill is going to come due, and news of the next installment comes via yet another telephone call to him at work: Janice wants to buy school clothes and the like for Nelson, and will do so to extravagant excess. Through this all, the encounter with Buchanan and the call from Janice, Rabbit's Linotyping tragicomically goes all to hell as he tries to set in type an account of old days in Brewer, dating all the way back to the Whiskey Rebellion of 1799. Updike shows the story set in type, section by section, with ruined lines included along with their corrected replacements, suggesting how much all of this is throwing Rabbit off his stride. Eventually he produces mostly gibberish.

Jill's relationship with Rabbit is rocky, Rabbit's mother is still in failing health (and still worrying about him), and Rabbit's father is aging and worrying about break-ins in the old neighborhood. Janice takes Nelson shopping as summer ends, opening new charge accounts at every store and buying expensive clothes, including a tailored suit rather than the blue jeans and Che Guevara sweatshirt that Nelson really wants. The new charge accounts are in Rabbit's name, of course, the bills will come to him, and the Saturday of shopping also means that he and Nelson cannot accompany Jill on her excursion to Valley Forge, the famous Revolutionary War site where the Continental Army spent the starving winter of 1777–78, to see where George Washington slept. When she returns, she and Rabbit argue and make love, and he not too truthfully says that he loves her—and then they cry together.

> He pulls her down to him, puts their cheeks together, so their tears will mix.
> Jill asks him, "Why are you crying?"
> "Why are you?"
> "Because the world is so shitty and I'm part of it."
> "Do you think there's a better one?"
> "There must be."
> "Well," he considers, "why the hell not?" (177)

Nelson finally comes home to show off his inappropriate and expensive clothes bought on Rabbit's dime. Rabbit's summer idyll truly is over, and reality is about to come pressing in.

Movies and Television

Movies and television are a motif in *Rabbit Redux* as in many others of Updike's work as he attempts to render the feel of particular years. (In Jack De Bellis's *The John Updike Encyclopedia* the list of films and film personalities mentioned in Updike's works covers eleven double-column pages.) Updike often works to associate particular productions with particular characters. Thus the presence of Kubrick's *2001: A Space Odyssey* in the novel echoes the moon landing of 1969 and also sends readers into its imagined future of space travel and the evolution of the human race. Nelson Angstrom, himself an almost-teen work in progress, is particularly entranced by the film. It depicts a not entirely optimistic future. A mysterious black monolith advances human evolution at key points. Human consciousness is imagined to have begun in prehistory when a protohuman ape touches the monolith and discovers that a bone can be used as a weapon; during a mission to Jupiter to intercept another monolith, Dr. Dave Bowman (blandly played by Keir Dullea) faces a sentient but murderously paranoid computer, HAL (the acronym is formed by taking the name of the computer corporation giant IBM and moving each letter back one space in the alphabet). When it turns malevolent, Bowman kills the machine, pulling one circuit after another from its memory banks as it reverts to a childhood state and then oblivion. Bowman arrives at the giant monolith and evolves himself, aging to senility and then becoming an infant of the next stage of humanity.

In contrast, during their sleepover Nelson and Billy Fosnacht watch *The Longest Day* (1962), the story of the heroic and costly D-Day Allied landing in Normandy, June 6, 1944, during World War II. Though considered innovative at the time of its release for using subtitled original languages rather than accented English to convey the dialogue of non-English-speaking characters, it was one of the last big-budget films to be shot in black and white and has an old-style cast of dozens of stars ranging from John Wayne to Richard Burton. Nelson, unclear on the historical time lines, asks his father if he was present on D-Day, but in 1944 Rabbit was Nelson's age. Rabbit's war was Korea, though he spent his army tour of duty in Texas. His military career was decidedly nonheroic.

Another throwback film invoked in *Rabbit Redux* is William Wyler's *Funny Girl* (1968), which Rabbit's mother is watching on television late in the novel. It stars Barbra Streisand in the musical comedy/drama adaptation to film of a 1964 Broadway production, the story of vaudeville, radio, and movie star Fanny Brice (1891–1951), who was famous as the character Baby Snooks. Mary Angstrom perhaps sees her own impending mortality in Brice's relatively short lifespan. Mary dies at around age sixty-eight in 1972, between the end of this novel and the beginning of the next.

Television shows mentioned in *Rabbit Redux* include *The Carol Burnett Show, Rowan and Martin's Laugh-In,* and *The Dating Game.* The first two were highly creative sketch comedy shows, while the third was a hackneyed combination of double-entendre humor and 1960s flower-power kitsch. It seems appropriate that Janice and Rabbit watch *The Dating Game* as they reconcile at the novel's end. Its question-and-answer format suggests the possibility of communication between the sexes, but the episodic format also suggested that this communication was tenuous. The parallels to the Angstroms' marriage were probably not difficult for readers of the time to grasp. Television is depicted in the novel as providing an eye into the unsettling realities of American life. An important example of this is when Rabbit comes home from work in the novel's third section to find Skeeter, Jill, and Nelson sitting together on the sofa and watching the evening news, an ironic version of the normal-seeming families around the nation who were also being exposed to all the disputes of the day

Skeeter is the snake in Rabbit and Jill's Garden of Eden, reappearing in the novel's third section to provide a knowledge of American class realities that makes their idyll at first difficult and then impossible, and leading to Jill's death in the fourth and final section of the book. Skeeter gives Rabbit lessons in black history and point of view, exposing him to such classics as Frederick Douglass's autobiography. A Vietnam veteran, Skeeter also calls into question Rabbit's easy, unthinking faith in America's benevolent presence throughout the world. He educates Rabbit on the evils of colonialism and the point of view of 1960s left-wing groups such as SDS and the Black Panthers. (Updike similarly fictionally incorporates a bomb-making accident involving the SDS-offshoot group the Weather Underground in *The Witches of Eastwick*.)

Skeeter arrives in September, having jumped bail after a police raid on Jimbo's Friendly Place that also netted Babe for possession of marijuana. He has become "one hot item . . . one *baad* niggeh," in his own words (179–80). In reality he may not be such as he claims. Rabbit discovers him sitting in an armchair in his living room. Jill wants to put him up for a few nights, but Rabbit sees him as pure evil.

> "Why are you doing this to me?" he asks of Jill.
> She turns her head, gives him that long-chinned profile, a dime's worth. "I was stupid," she says, "to think that you might trust me. You shouldn't have said you loved me."
> Skeeter hums "True Love," the old Crosby–Grace Kelly single. (181–82)

Throughout the rest of the novel, Skeeter serves similarly as a disruptive and ironic commentator on Rabbit's straightforward, innocent view of American reality. He calls Rabbit "Chuck" (a diminutive and dismissive version of the black characterization of oppressive whites as "Mr. Charlie") and rejects Jill's attempts at follow feeling. Despite supposedly having been "screwing her all afternoon," he tells her he "wouldn't take you on a bet, you poor cock-happy bitch. Skeeter splits alone" (182).

When Skeeter successively insults Rabbit's parents and God, calling himself "black Jesus," Rabbit is filled with "a creeping sweetness, rage. . . . Sunday school images—a dead man whiter than lilies, the lavender rocks where he was betrayed by a kiss—are being revived in him" (183). Enraged, he punches Skeeter again and again, "packed so solid with anger and fear he is seeing with his pores" (183). Instead of responding in kind, though, the younger man collapses to the floor and cocoons himself. Skeeter is weaker than he seems. When

Nelson and Billy burst in, alarmed at the sounds of conflict, Rabbit relents and tells Nelson that Skeeter will be staying a while.

Jill proves to be monumentally heedless of money and values, hugely privileged and clueless even though simultaneously an appealing and searching soul. She ruins her Porsche sports car and sells it for six hundred dollars. She contributes to her own destruction, echoing the destruction of conventional American society by the social and cultural forces of the 1960s. Rabbit is also implicated in her death and in larger changes. By hosting Jill and Skeeter and evoking the wrath of his neighbors, he helps to bring about a conflagration that destroys his house and her life. As Updike depicts the state of the nation, it was an open question at the time whether the United States would survive and continue to evolve.

Later in the novel, while Rabbit is sleeping with Peggy Fosnacht, he gets a call from Skeeter saying that something is wrong at home. He borrows Peggy's car and drive to Penn Villas to find his home burned and Jill dead, again a reflection of the seemingly anarchic violence of the time. The police suspiciously question Rabbit about what seems to be a case of arson but eventually decide that the jails are full enough without adding a solid citizen such as he. They also suspect Skeeter, but when he reappears after the police have left, he identifies the arsonists to Rabbit as two white men from the neighborhood. Rabbit surreptitiously drives Skeeter out of town, gives him the thirty dollars that are in his wallet, and even shakes his hand in farewell.

> Skeeter tells him, "Never did figure your angle."
>
> "Probably wasn't one," is the answer. . . . As Harry backs Peggy's Fury around in the strait intersection, the young black waits by a bank of brown weed stalks. In the rearview mirror, Skeeter looks oddly right, blends right in, even with the glasses and the goatee, hanging empty-handed between fields of stubble where crows settle and shift, gleaming. (292–93)

The fourth and final section of *Rabbit Redux* opens with Rabbit typesetting the news of Jill's death and the destruction of his own house in Penn Villas. It will be his last article, for he is interrupted by his boss's bringing news that Verity's new offset press is arriving at week's end and that his union seniority is too low for him to be retrained on the new machine. His father will continue, even Buchanan will do so, but Rabbit is too young and will be left with a couple of month's severance pay and his boss's advice that he leave the county and start over somewhere else. Rabbit's 1960s are turning out to embody the worst fears of Middle America. In his father's words, "The whole economy's scared. Nixon's getting himself to be the new Hoover, these moratorium doves'll be begging for LBJ to come back before Tricky Dick's got done giving their bank accounts a squeeze!" (298). Thus it is appropriate that the patriotic Columbus

Day parade Rabbit later drives through on the way to his burned house to look for Skeeter's wallet and Jill's missing six hundred dollars is "a four-color nightmare of martial music, throbbing exhaustion, bare-thighed girls twirling bolts of lightning, iridescent drummers pounding a tattoo on the taut hollow of Harry's stomach" (298).

Still later Rabbit meets Jill's mother and stepfather at the police station when they arrive in the aftermath of the fire. Rabbit is afraid of what she might ask of him but discovers that she is of "his generation," and so "he could understand what she wanted . . . to stay out of harm's way . . . to have some fun and not be blamed." By contrast "Jill had been too old for him, too wise, having been born so much later" (302).

Leading Rabbit back outside after the interview with Jill's mother, the police chief absolves him of any guilt in Jill's death: "'Rich bitch. If she'd given the girl half a reason to stay home she'd be alive today. I see things like this every week. All our bad checks are being cashed. Keep your nose clean, Angstrom, and take care of your own.' A coach's paternal punch on the arm, and Harry was sent back into the world" (303). The image recalls coach Marty Tothero, Rabbit's mentor in *Rabbit, Run:* reassuring, traditional, and a part of the sort of order that Rabbit always seeks, even if it seems evanescent and of the past during the time period in which the novel is set.

The final major event of *Rabbit Redux* is the return of Rabbit's sister, Mim, who comes home from Las Vegas driving an Oldsmobile Toronado, an ostentatiously trendy luxury car of the time. The Toronado is huge and white, the same color as Jill's diminutive Porsche. "A guy lent it to me," she says with a sigh when her father asks where she got it (307).

The reader comes to understand that Mim has become a prostitute. She has had her buckteeth fixed but not her bulbous nose, which "saves her face from looking like others and gives it, between the peacock eyes and the actress-fussy mouth, a lenient homeliness" (306). There is still something authentic about Mim, and Rabbit's father reminisces about how close his daughter and son were and about the private language the two of them shared. Rabbit cannot remember that language, if it even existed, but he remembers their togetherness. Mim's knowing pragmatism about human relationships makes her a good adviser on the subject of Janice: she sees that Janice's affair with Stavros was "the first step she's taken since she drowned the baby." Mim understands that Janice is like a child who has grabbed the candy inside a jar and cannot pull her hand out but refuses to let go: "She wants the idea of what she's made out of the candy in her own mind. So. Somebody has to break the jar for her." When Rabbit says, "I don't want her back still in love with this greaseball," she responds, "That's just how you have to take her" (310).

Brother and sister discuss the lessons Rabbit has learned under Skeeter's tutelage. "I learned . . . this country isn't perfect," he concludes, reductively but with conviction (311). They also discuss Mim's life in Las Vegas, and she tries to describe its gangster bosses but concludes that Rabbit will not understand them or the rules by which one lives in the desert, where the sun is an enemy and "anything free has a rattlesnake under it" (312). She sees Rabbit and her father as soft by comparison but Janice as "hard as a nut," something Mim had not liked about her previously but feels that she would like now, after her own experiences of Las Vegas. She warns Rabbit that the whole country is going to be getting harder, but later in the novel, she tells him something a little different, that "people want to be nice. . . . They don't like being shits, that much; but you have to find some way out of it for them. You have to help them" (326).

In that spirit Mim seems to take charge of returning Janice to Rabbit; in the process she matter-of-factly sleeps with Stavros three times (only three, in keeping with one of her rules for interaction with men to avoid troublesome commitments). Mim also pays attention to those around her. She is the only one to remember Nelson's upcoming thirteenth birthday, and knowing exactly what he would appreciate—a minibike, of course—she buys it for him, arranging for it to be delivered to the Fosnachts' apartment building and to be stored there so that Nelson and Billy can play with it together. She announces this to Rabbit the day before the birthday, in the rain, as they shoot baskets together. "The poor kid deserves *some*thing for what you put him through," she tells him, and he calls her a "super aunt." She replies, "And you're so dumb that you don't even know it's raining" (327), perhaps a reference to the line "You don't need a weather man to know which way the wind blows" from Bob Dylan's song "Subterranean Homesick Blues" (1965), which became something of a counter-culture anthem of the 1960s. Readers of the time likely would have caught the allusion—and considered whether Rabbit had really learned anything permanent in the school of Skeeter.

As the novel nears its end, it enters the minds of Rabbit and Janice. He lies alone in bed night after night, masturbating to one imagined partner and another, even imagining in great detail Mim and Stavros together, but no fantasy is satisfactory until Jill returns, more like a ghost than a memory, and all her little imperfections that "slightly repelled him . . . become the body of his memory" (330). He then sees Jill and Skeeter together, joined, and when he comes closer "to be a father and lover to them, . . . they fly apart like ink and paper whirling to touch for an instant on the presses. . . . Waking to find his hand in empty mid-air he cries; Grief rises in him" (331). At last Rabbit cries for Jill and resolves to tell Nelson that she had visited him again.

Meanwhile Janice resents Stavros's having slept with Mim. In bed with him but unable to sleep, she reflects on the perfection of her lovemaking with him, approached previously only by what the movies had tried to tell her about sex. She realizes that she had "failed to extract testimony that his sense of their love was as absolute as her own" (333). In fact Stavros is ready for her to go back to Rabbit, which fills her with rage. Later she awakens to the sound of Stavros experiencing an attack of angina. Janice cannot find the nitroglycerine pills he asks her to bring from the bathroom, but she presses against him instead. She brings a gift of life in this instance but also realizes that she brings too much disorder to Stavros's life: "This love that has blown through her has been a miracle, the one thing worthy of it remaining is to leave. Spirits are insatiable but bodies get enough. She has had enough, he has had enough, more might be too much. . . . Janice sees that in the vast volume of her love she has renounced the one possible imperfection, its object. Her own love engulfs her; she sinks down through its purity swiftly fallen, all feathers" (337). Icarus-like, Janice has flown too close to the sun of her love for Stavros, and now the affair is over.

In the novel's denouement, Janice leaves Stavros, Ollie and Peggy Fosnacht get back together, and Rabbit's mother continues to decline, though she is nicer to Janice now when they talk on the phone. Eventually Rabbit and Janice meet at their half-burned and now graffiti-covered house on Vista Crescent. It is worth a lot: $11,000 settlement from the insurance company, and $19,500 as is for the wreck from an interested buyer. They decide to sell and shake hands on the deal, and Rabbit drives Janice back toward her mother's house on Joseph Street, where she now is staying while contemplating moving with Nelson into the same high rise as Peggy Fosnacht. They do not get to Joseph Street, however. Janice and Rabbit stop at the aptly named Safe Haven Motel, watch a little of *The Dating Game*, which Updike describes as oddly tinted and distorted by bad reception on the color TV, just in case readers might miss the practical and emotional significance of their reunion. Janice insists that they share a bed, though there are two available in the motel room. They undress somewhat awkwardly but also with familiarity. They do not make love but drift off to sleep together, nestled familiarly, "the motel room long and secret as a burrow" (353). It seems at least for the moment that Rabbit is safe again.

If there is a flaw to this second novel, it is that Updike still is developing his approach to his characters, and perhaps that he is trying a little too hard to represent the late 1960s, pouring into the novel a lot of subject matter rather far from his own experience, including the presence of Skeeter, who improbably comes to live with Rabbit in Janice's absence. As a result there is sometimes a raw quality to this novel, in contrast to the usually smooth and assured style of Updike's narration. But there is a lot that was raw in the period, and there is a lot in the novel that is smoothly written and observed. Rabbit has engaged with—or perhaps only flirted with—the passions and concerns of the late 1960s, but he has returned again to his stable, middle-class, ordinary reality. He is still jobless, but Janice can support the family with her position at Springer Motors.

"He. She. Sleeps. O.K.?" (353) are the last words of the novel. While Rabbit and Janice are back together and at rest, the novel appropriately ends on a question mark. Will things be OK for Rabbit and Janice, and for America? It is hard to tell, as particularly it was for the readers of 1970, but Rabbit has gone through a lot and come back to his comfortable if imperfect marriage.

Rabbit Is Rich

In *Rabbit Is Rich* (1981), Updike seems to hit his stride in terms of comfort with his characters and with their presentation in his multidecade project representing American change and continuity. That he is working again with characters in their small-town milieu adds to his command of his material. He does not stretch beyond what he knows and understands well; however, this is not a weakness in the novel, rather one of its huge strengths. *Rabbit Is Rich* was the most positively reviewed novel in the tetralogy, and the one that won the most literary prizes. It is a work in which the passage of time and the changes time can bring are strongly in evidence, adding poignancy and resonance to the narration.

Rabbit walks back into his own past in the novel. Two decades after the events of *Rabbit, Run,* he actually *has* a past beyond his old high school basketball experiences. While not a particularly contemplative character, he seeks out and reacts to stimuli, and Updike presents him with several opportunities. The first major stimulus is the visit of a customer to the Springer Motors Toyota lot. Rabbit has returned to sales after losing his job at Verity Press, and selling Toyotas has made Rabbit rich—or really made Janice's mother rich, and by extension him and Janice. They live with Janice's mother in her house on Joseph Street, and while Rabbit does not own the Toyota agency, he feels that he does and is pleased. Following the death of his father-in-law, he became "the man up front" at the dealership (2).

The reader learns early in the novel that Skeeter is apparently dead at the hands of the Philadelphia police; the tumult of Black Power and the counter-culture seen in the previous novel has disappeared. Rabbit's preferred normality seems to have returned, except that that the United States is suffering through an oil crisis resulting from the aftermath of the Islamic Revolution in Iran, which overthrew the U.S. puppet, the Shah. The oil crisis has put the dealership in a fortuitous position as the seller of the most fuel-efficient vehicles available to consumers. This makes Rabbit extremely happy, even though his high school basketball clippings are fading and yellowing beside his office door, sealed under glass (2). Time's movement cannot be resisted, but something almost as good as sports stardom has come to him. The novel begins on the first days of summer, optimistically, reminiscent of the ending of *Rabbit, Run,* in which the first days of summer 1959 included the death and funeral of Rabbit's infant daughter.

A young man and his girlfriend come in to look at cars. Charlie Stavros, still a salesman at the dealership, calls them hicks, but Rabbit feels somehow protective of them as they warily enter. With "Charlie's snipe ringing in his ear" (10), he takes on the two, sizing them up in a beautifully written passage that reveals a good deal more about the young woman than Rabbit suspects.

> The boy could be just scouting out prices for his father, and the girlfriend be riding along, or not even be girlfriend, but a sister, or a hitchhiker. A little touch of the hooker about her looks. The way her soft body wants to spill from these small clothes, the faded denim shorts and purple Paisley halter. The shining faintly freckled flesh of her shoulders and her top arms and the busy wanton abundance of her browny-red many-colored hair, carelessly bundled. *A buried bell rings.* She has deep blue eyes in deep sockets and the silence of a girl from the country used to letting men talk while she holds a sweet-and-sour secret in her mouth, sucking it. . . . This girl will not stick with this boy. Rabbit wants this to be so; he imagines he feels an unwitting swimming of her spirit up toward his, while her manner is all stillness. He feels she wants to hide from him, but is too big and white, too suddenly womanly, too nearly naked. . . . She is bruisable, he wants to protect her; he relieves her of the pressure of his gaze, too long by a second. (11; emphasis added)

Characteristic of Rabbit, his gaze begins as sexual but reveals something more subtle and intuitive. One might argue that this exquisitely sensual description is more Updike's style than Rabbit's, but Rabbit's perceptiveness and openness to experience are part of what makes him so appealing a character and such an appropriate vehicle for Updike's decades-long project in the tetralogy.

Rabbit's sales talk runs smoothly. He touts in turn the advantages of each of the different Toyotas on display as the young man notices them, running a soft sell so as not to chase the couple away. As "generous paternal talkativeness keeps bubbling up in Harry" (13), Updike provides a neat hint at where this is going. They test drive a blue Corolla at Stavros's suggestion, since he also wants to get Rabbit out of the showroom so he can complete some paperwork in peace. Rabbit seems talkative and happy, as he often is in his most appealing moments. He is "floating—on their youth, on his money, on the brightness of this June afternoon and its promise that tomorrow, a Sunday, will be fair for his golf game" (14). Mingled with these simple pleasures, however, is his crassly sexual view of the young woman, such that maintaining his appeal to the reader is a considerable feat on the part of Updike. At one point during the test drive, he looks at her and "imagines he smells vanilla," which leads him to think up obscene flavors for Sealtest ice cream (17). Such passages illustrate Updike's role as a chronicler of American sexuality and his tendency to push the envelope in terms of freedom of expression, though some readers find them tiresome.

During the test drive, Rabbit intuits that the young woman actually is his daughter by Ruth Leonard, though she evades his sly questions to try to confirm this and even his attempt to learn her name.

In a wonderful scene, Rabbit's mind moves swiftly through his thoughts about the United States in 1979, the changes in Brewer, and how Springer Motors used to operate when used cars were its only sales. Now that Rabbit has a past that sentimentally colors his perceptions, nostalgia is a larger element in this novel, as indeed nostalgia seems a stronger and stronger element as Updike moves through his career, perhaps inevitably for someone so tied to his and his characters' impressions of particular times and places. Nostalgia suffuses this novel, particularly in its ending, which circles back to the question of Rabbit's daughter.

Relationships with women are at the center of the novel generally, not just Rabbit's but also the less than satisfactory relationships of his less than satisfactory son, Nelson, a Kent State University student. Nelson has returned from an excursion to Colorado not with his slightly older girlfriend, Pru (a former secretary who is carrying his baby and using purloined Kent State stationery to type daily letters that mostly annoy him), but with their friend Melanie, a disciple of early twentieth-century Russian mystic and world traveler George Ivanovich Gurdjieff. Melanie has access to "realms real to others but not real to [Nelson]—not just languages he didn't know, or theorems he couldn't grasp, but drifting areas of unprofitable knowledge where nevertheless profits of a sort were being made." She is a part of the grown-up world, "smugly smiling out at him from within that bubble where the mystery resided that amounted to power" (133). Confusingly for Nelson, she dates Charlie Stavros and lives at Janice's mother's house. She wants Nelson to follow Gurdjieff's "Fourth Way" of mystical Christianity in order to expand his consciousness, but at this point in his life, he lacks a consciousness to expand. He more prosaically wishes to go out to a new bar, the Laid-Back, with his public school buddy Billy. By midnovel, however, Pru arrives from Colorado, and she and Nelson marry. Stavros is (temporarily, as it turns out) put out to pasture so that Nelson can take over his sales job at the dealership. Though Rabbit strenuously objects to Nelson's abandoning his college degree when so close to its completion, in this as in other matters, Janice and her mother rule. They are the actual owners of the dealership.

Late in the novel, Rabbit and Janice take a seven-day vacation trip to an un-identified Caribbean island with two other couples, Webb and Cindy Murkett (respectively the oldest and youngest of the group), and Ronnie and Thelma Harrison, their trip bankrolled by a month's profit from Rabbit and Janice's speculating in silver bullion. Such speculation is one of the many middle-class fads of the time that Updike documents. The profit also has helped finance the purchase of a new house, into which they move late in the novel, escaping at least for a while the house on Joseph Street, although it remains at the center of the novels, an ambiguous symbol both of continuity and of stasis.

Rabbit has been watching Cindy Murkett for much of this novel, and his main motive for the trip is to enter into her "secret places, of folds and fur and moist membranes where a diaphragm can go . . . his certain destination" (356). Compared to Cindy, he thinks, Janice is still "the dumb mutt," laughing at Ronnie's crass characterizing of their first breath of tropical air as "better than a blow job" (357). Cindy grows tanner, plumper, and more appealing to Rabbit as the days pass, while the stodgy Thelma sits "swaddled and watchful," avoid-ing sunburn (359), and Janice continues to annoy him.

Late in their vacation week, with the vacationers a little bored with their routine of swimming, eating, and daily golf for the men, Rabbit loses three hundred dollars at roulette while Ronnie ends up eight hundred dollars ahead. The two have competed since Rabbit was the star of the high-school basketball court and Ronnie was always trying to catch up. At the end of the evening, Rabbit has sex with Janice "out of general irritation" since his play for Cindy has come to naught. The closest he gets to her is during an excursion in a tiny rented Sunfish, the generic and widely popular boat for beginning sailors. His fear of sharks and lack of knowledge of sailing make the whole a less than satisfactory experience. Finally they tip the boat, and Cindy abandons him, slipping his attempted embrace in the water, righting the sailboat, and taking it up onto the beach without him. A Sunfish in a somewhat similar situation also appears in Rabbit at Rest, illustrating Updike's characteristic pattern of echo-ing images and occurrences throughout the tetralogy.

As the vacation draws to a close, the couples decide on wife swapping "done with affection and respect" (369), in the ironic words of Webb Murkett, though there is considerable suggestion that it is the women who actually have cooked this up. The couples split up into their new configurations as the resort band appropriately plays "Send in the Clowns." Rabbit "hears Cindy giggle, at a distance, for it is not her hand with such gentle determination pulling him along, but Thelma's" (371). It turns out that the women have decided Harry can have Cindy the next night, but first he will sleep with Thelma. Thelma, a "thin-faced sallow woman he scarcely knows" (372), loves him. Janice had guessed this long before, and in fact did not invite Thelma to Nelson's wedding because of it. The lovemaking of Thelma and Rabbit is complicated by her period and the intimation that she is ill, perhaps with a cancer that makes every other month's period a trial for her, but she is determined to please him, for reasons she explains:

> "Janice and Cindy noticed. They knew you were who I'd want."
>
> "Uh—not to, you know, milk this, but what is it about me that turns you on?"
>
> "Oh, darling. Everything. Your height and the way you move, as if you're still a skinny twenty-five. The way you never sit down anywhere without making sure there's a way out. Your little provisional smile, like a little boy at some party where the bullies might get him the next minute. Your good humor. You believe in people so—Webb, you hang on to his words where nobody else pays attention, and Janice, you're so proud of her it's pathetic. . . . You're so grateful to be anywhere, you think that tacky [golf] club and that hideous house of Cindy's are heaven. It's wonderful. You're so glad to be alive." (379)

This is as much Updike explaining his protagonist to readers as Thelma explaining her love to Rabbit, but as she revels in his presence he, having been sucked and having screwed her in the ass (her idea, to offer him something he hasn't gotten from anyone else), still is left feeling that he is looking into the void. But he speaks to Thelma as to no one else about his life, particularly regarding his disappointment in his son and his thoughts that he might have a daughter and "that there was something that wanted him to find it, that he was here on earth on a kind of assignment" (379), possibly an evocation of his religious sense. Despite the depth of their conversation, Rabbit does not appreciate a mature, intelligent, and thoughtful woman such as Thelma; instead he continues to pursue the superficially attractive and otherwise second-rate Cindy.

Ever-disappointing Nelson turns out to be the barrier between Rabbit and his anticipated night with Cindy. Janice learns that he has come up missing, having abandoned Pru somewhat as Rabbit abandoned Janice in *Rabbit, Run*. When Rabbit suggests that they deal with Nelson when they get home—their scheduled flight home is in a day and a half—he learns that Janice already has canceled their original tickets in a panic. He must go home without his hoped-for encounter with Cindy.

None of this makes Janice look good. She comes across as clueless, self-centered, and panicky. But Rabbit looks worse. He is not concerned with his son, does not empathize with his wife's concern over Nelson, and perhaps most tellingly does not really react to learning that Thelma loves him or discovering that she is a sympathetic confidante. Only Cindy seems to have meaning for him, not the people who actually are a part of his life and who might provide it with meaning.

Still searching, late in the novel he goes to visit his old lover, Ruth, on her farm—she is now the widowed Ruth Byer. (There is a faint suggestion that her relationship to her husband somewhat echoed the biblical story of Ruth and Boaz, with the farm a refuge for Ruth, as Boaz's farm was for the biblical Ruth.) Rabbit repeatedly visits the farm over the course of the novel, lurking unseen nearby but unable to steel himself to a confrontation with this figure from his past. Ruth is as solid as when he knew her years before, now gone to fat but "still tall, compared to Janice, compared to any of the women of his life but Mim and his mother." "The hall inside smells decidedly of the past, the way these old farm houses do" (398), when Rabbit and Ruth finally meet. One suspects that Updike's memory of the farmhouse in which he lived during his teenage years is also playing its role in the emotional resonance of the scene. Updike indeed is a master of memory.

Even face to face with Rabbit, Ruth will not confirm his suspicion about their daughter Annabelle. Ruth claims that their child was aborted in those days before abortion became legal. She and Rabbit dance around Annabelle's paternity, Ruth not wanting to give anything away, Rabbit unwilling to press the matter, until he finds himself maneuvered out the door, she having avoided his intended goodbye peck on her cheek. "By the time he has taken a step off the concrete porch, her shadow has vanished from the double door's black glass. The gray of the day has intensified, releasing a few dry flakes of snow that will not amount to anything, that float sideways like flecks of ash," suggesting the evanescence of their past connection in the novel's present time and again suggesting mortality to the reader. Rabbit decides, "Let it go. Let it go. God doesn't want him to have a daughter" (408–9). The matter of Annabelle and her parentage recurs a decade later in *Rabbit at Rest* and roughly two decades later in *Rabbit Remembered,* continuing to weave patterns of connection and meaning across time.

Something else makes Rabbit forget his encounter with Ruth. Meeting Janice after lunch, he finds her now a more appealing partner than the taciturn and recalcitrant (though more intelligent) Ruth. Janice "looks petite and prosperous and, with her Caribbean tan, younger than forty-three. . . . She hardly listens to his lie, is breathy and electric with news of her own." Nelson has been found in Ohio and has returned to college at Kent State. Rabbit has a wife suited to him, one who will not question or intrude—or even think very much—but he still thinks of "old Ruth" and "the idiotic thought, which it seems he should bottle and sell, that our tears are always young, the saltwater stays the same from cradle, as she says, to grave" (408).

Now affluent, Janice and Rabbit have bought their own home in a mature suburb built up in the 1940s, and they move up to upscale Penn Park in January, leaving behind Mrs. Springer and Pru (and Pru's new baby, due out of the hospital) for life on a cul-de-sac at 14½ Franklin Drive. (In *Rabbit Redux* they had lived only in Penn Villas, the less affluent neighboring subdivision nearer to the city center.) The novel ends in their sparsely furnished new house on the day of Super Bowl XIV, Sunday, January 20, 1980. Characteristically for Updike, the particular day and popular culture event suggests meanings in the novel. Rabbit is hoping for a Pittsburgh Steelers loss after watching the halftime show from the Rose Bowl, an exercise in 1940s WWII nostalgia, but the novel ends before the game does. Thus he is left in process, without knowing the game's result—though of course the reader can know it (the Los Angeles Rams won, 31–19). Janice's mother arrives late, bringing along Pru and Nelson's new baby. The child, a girl, is deposited on Rabbit's lap as he sits in front of his brand-new Sony television: "Rabbit hates to put any more money into Japanese pockets but he knows from *Consumer Reports* that in this particular line they can't be touched for quality" (410). His perceptions, and Updike's evocation of them, are front and center as he holds the child: "You can feel in the curve of the cranium she's feminine, that shows from the first day. Through all this she has pushed to be here, in his lap, his hands, a real presence hardly weighing anything but alive. Fortune's hostage, heart's desire, a granddaughter. His. Another nail in his coffin. His" (423). The tentative "O.K.?" of the preceding novel's ending has become a more affirmative "His" at the end of *Rabbit Is Rich*.

Rabbit indeed is rich, not only in a monetary sense, though there is some doubt that he really understands this. The new baby seems to have arrived partly to balance the absence of his own daughters, Becky lost to death and Annabelle as yet unconfirmed to him. He is as rich in many ways as he ever will be. In the next novel in the tetralogy that affluence will be tested in the form of a risk to the life of his granddaughter.

Rabbit at Rest

The last novel in the Rabbit tetralogy, *Rabbit at Rest* (1990), is suffused by death, as indeed all of these novels have human mortality as their one great continuing thematic concern. Rabbit dies an untimely death in this novel—he is only in his mid-50s—but there is the sense that perhaps he has burned himself out, unwilling to adapt fully to the changing American landscape, in which he seems less and less to fit, and still running from commitments and anything else that frightens him. He also has been unable to adapt to the changes of aging and has not taken care of his health. In this he is perhaps also a representative American. Much of the novel is concerned with the state of Rabbit's heart, a physiological condition that allows for a parallel symbolic exploration of his emotions, loves, and relationships.

Much of the novel is set during an eventful week between Christmas and New Year in 1988. The story begins the Tuesday after Christmas, in Florida, where Rabbit and Janice are living for the winter in Valhalla Village, ironically named as neither character is particularly heroic and their life is hardly paradisiacal. They engage in typical tourist activities, including a visit to Thomas Edison's Florida home and workshop in Fort Myers, but the most significant of these is another ocean sailing excursion. In a second Sunfish accident, Rabbit overturns a rented sailboat after going too far out from shore and has to rescue his granddaughter, Judy, from under its sail. He has a heart attack during the event. The description of the episode seems dislocated from the actual experience, partly because Rabbit's heart attack grows progressively more severe, but more significantly because he remains unable to connect vitally with those around him, even as he watches his beloved granddaughter, "this perfect female child, all coppery and bright and as yet unmarred" (117), almost drown. When the boat turns over, she is trapped under the sail, and Rabbit strives to rescue her in a masterfully-written scene that goes on for pages with an immediacy that exemplifies Updike's command of style and of Rabbit's point of view.

> He has never been a natural swimmer. Air, light, water, silence all clash inside his head in a thunderous demonstration of mercilessness. Even in this instant of perfectly dense illumination there is space for his lifelong animal distaste for putting his head underwater, and for the thought that another second of doing nothing might miraculously bring it all right; the child's smiling face will surface with saltwater sparkling in her eyelashes. But the noon sun says now or never and something holy in him screams that all can be retrieved and he opens his mouth and sucks down panicked breath through a sieve of pain in his chest and tries to burrow though a resistant opacity where he cannot see or breathe. (118–19)

As Rabbit pulls Judy out from under the sail, "he realizes that her fright has its limits; she thinks that even out here nothing more drastic than discomfort can befall her. She has a child's sense of immortality and he is its guardian" (120). Despite his crassness, bad jokes, and self-centered thoughts, he manages in the moment to stay focused on his granddaughter and achieves something close to heroism, as close as he might be able to come. As in his high school sports career, it is physical action that defines the best in him.

Remembering Cindy Murkett's actions at the previous capsizing, he manages to right the Sunfish despite the pain in his chest, "a red internal blaze" (122), and he has Judy sing to him—"Row, Row, Row Your Boat" to start with—to make sure he stays conscious. They make their way back to the beach—first to the accompaniment of nursery rhymes sung in her child's voice and then to commercial jingles for Oscar Mayer wieners, Toyota, and Coke as Judy runs out of nursery rhymes, and then to songs from movie musicals, *The Wizard of Oz* and *Snow White and the Seven Dwarfs*. Rabbit feels himself to be "a piece of physical luggage to be delivered into the hands of others," yet he feels "good, down deep" (125). Coming to shore, he lies on the sand, "like a jellyfish washed up, bulging, tremblingly full of a desire for its lost element" (27); he is taken to the hospital, where a cardiac catheterization reveals the state of his heart: not good.

Returning to Pennsylvania in April, Rabbit finds intimations that Nelson has been defrauding the Springer Motors Toyota dealership. Pru reveals to him something of Nelson's problems—cocaine addiction and wife beating in addition to embezzlement—and Janice soon learns more.

Meanwhile Rabbit has his continuing heart issues, and he checks into St. Joseph's Hospital for five days for an angioplasty to clear a blockage in a coronary artery. This was a new and cutting-edge procedure at the time of the novel. Fortuitously, Annabelle is one of Rabbit's nurses. She suggests that he meet Ruth, with whom she is again living, but Rabbit begs off, pleading that he feels "fat and a medical mess" (265). "Tell your mother if she asks, that maybe we'll meet some other time," he says, but what he thinks is, "under the pear trees, in Paradise" (266).

Janice's news about Nelson is another blow. She has confirmed that he has embezzled thousands of dollars from the dealership to pay for crack cocaine, by writing checks made out to cash, selling used cars at a discount and pocketing the difference, and underreporting sales to Toyota Motor Credit Corporation. Updike's research into the automobile business, careful as usual, is demonstrated in the primer on dealer fraud he neatly slips into the narration. The total amount Nelson has stolen remains unknown, since his new accountant and accomplice, Lyle, a gay man supposedly in remission from AIDS but obviously in failing health, resists Rabbit's inquiries into the apparent lack of used car sales on the statements sent him in Florida and then "accidentally" erases computer disks. During their strained conversation, Lyle sidesteps queries and holds out for authorization directly from Nelson or Janice to show Rabbit the sales figures.

Soon Rabbit finds himself fielding dunning calls from Nelson's cocaine dealers, "grainy voices with that rich timbre peculiar to black males" with names such as Julius, Luther, Perry, or Dave, and then from someone with a foreign accent who threatens harm to Nelson "or even to certain of his near and dear" (207), "leaving Harry with the sensation that the walls of his solid little limestone house are as thin as diet crackers, that the wall-to-wall carpet under his feet is soaked with water, that a pipe has burst and there is no plumber to call" (208). These disembodied voices have intruded into Rabbit's comfortable world as did Skeeter in *Rabbit Redux*.

Facing the threat of prosecution, Nelson consents to ninety days of live-in rehab in Philadelphia, to begin before the disgusted Rabbit returns from the hospital and has to see him. Rabbit will resume running the dealership, despite his plea that he is a "sick son of a bitch," at Charlie Stavros's suggestion. Despite Rabbit's suspicion that Stavros and Janice have resumed their love affair, she protests that he is "just an old friend, who's been wonderful in this crisis" (273).

Rabbit's affair with Thelma Harrison also ends. She and Ronnie drop by his hospital room after her appointment for dialysis—her kidneys have shut down as an effect of her long-time illness, lupus. Earlier she had provided the first warning that Nelson might be spending thousands on his cocaine addiction. Now she asks Rabbit if he remembers the biblical book of Ecclesiastes: "A time to gather up stones, a time to cast them away? I'm beginning to think there's a time to give up" (278). Her ability to care for him is burning out with her life but not gone. Ronnie avoids the pain of Thelma's impending death by small talk, ironically calling Rabbit "the Old Master" (of the high school basketball court) and characteristically trying to sell him insurance—"some twenty-payment straight life. . . . Let me work up some figures." Given the state of Rabbit's health, it would have been a good purchase, for he says that he feels like "master of nothing at this point" (279).

Rabbit contemplates Thelma, and "all the afternoons when their bodies intertwined and exchanged fluids are not gone but safe inside him, his cells remembering." Again memory helps to define him. In front of Ronnie, Thelma asks for and receives an almost, but not quite, chaste kiss from Rabbit. Once she and Ronnie are gone, Rabbit again remembers her positively, "all soft and blurred by their lovemaking," but he also recalls his concealed "revulsion at his own smell on her lips" after oral sex (279).

On the day Pru drives Nelson to rehab in North Philadelphia and Janice brings Rabbit home from the hospital, he makes a typically unthinking misstep. It has been an eventful day, told mostly from Janice's point of view. She convinces Nelson that he indeed will go to jail if he skips rehab (which he is characterizing as a con job): "If I didn't love you . . . I'd let you go on destroying yourself," she finally asserts. "Her store of words is exhausted; she launches herself toward the white sneering face and embraces the boy, who grudgingly, after a resistant wriggle, responds and hugs her back" (287). In the evening she is scheduled to take a quiz in her real estate course, and against his objections she arranges for Rabbit to stay with her at her mother's house along with Pru and his two grandchildren so that he will not be left alone. Rabbit grudgingly goes along with the plan and spends some of the afternoon in one of Updike's characteristically nostalgic set-pieces, a walk through Mount Judge, popping nitroglycerin pills, remembering the way the town was when he was younger, and contrasting its new, yuppified present. The 1940s row house where Rabbit once lived with Janice, Nelson, and Becky now is repainted in brighter colors, with Camaros and BMWs parked on the street, the old dead-end street now extended to a row of new houses, and the view of downtown now fashionable rather than gritty and working-class. As elsewhere Rabbit is the reader's bridge to the past.

In the evening he watches TV with Pru and the children and snaps at Judy for channel hopping with the remote control when he wants to see the end of a *Cosby Show* rerun. Rabbit sees Claire Huxtable as "restoring decency" when her TV daughter and a friend lip sync "with a sexuality . . . startling and premature" but also as "implying that indecency is all right, in its place, its wise time, as in one of those mutually ogling Huxtable snuggles that end many a *Cosby Show.*" The ogling snuggle is the sort of detail that would attract Rabbit. A few moments later he criticizes Michael Jordan because his tongue lolls out as he goes up for a layup: "he's an intelligent guy, why does he swing his tongue around like an imbecile?" (306). There are few white players in the game, and Rabbit finds it "incredible" that he himself ever had been on a basketball court. Whatever he might have learned about sexuality, race, and envy from Jill and Skeeter in *Rabbit Redux* seems to have left him.

The children finally in bed, Judy apologized to for his outburst, Rabbit settles into his dead mother-in-law's bed, the light off, listening to rain and a "smothered concussion, distant thunder. . . . His heart is giving him no pain, just floats wounded on the sea of ebbing time" (309). Updike's description is evocative of Rabbit's position, lost in time and space, in the dark in many ways, both literal and metaphorical.

His evening is not over, however. Janice will still be at her real estate class for at least another hour and a quarter. Pru, wanting to talk, comes in, sits on the bed, and smokes. "I just need a little adult company," she says, launching into a discussion of Nelson's shortcomings. She describes him as a complete loser, "out all night doing God knows what, then this sniveling and begging for forgiveness afterwards" (311). Rabbit suggests that she knew what she was getting into when she married Nelson, but she asserts that she did not. Sex has also become a barrier between husband and wife:

"Then he gets sore and tells me what a cold fish I am. He means sex. A thing that goes fast with coke is shame; these women that are hooked will do anything. I say to him, you're not going to give me AIDS from one of your coke whores. So he goes out again. It's a vicious circle. It's been going on for years. (312)

'Maybe' two years ago Nelson became a big enough user on his own to need to steal. At first he just stole from us, money that would have gone into the house and stuff, and then he started stealing from you—the company. I hope you send him to jail, I really do." (312)

Her voice is hoarsening and finding a certain swing, a welling up. "I have no use for him any more. I'm scared to fuck him. I'm scared to be legally associated with him. I've wasted my life. You don't know what it's like. You're a man, you're free, you can do what you want in life, until you're at least sixty at least you're a buyer. A woman's a seller. She has to be. And she better not haggle too long. I'm thirty-three. I've had my shot, Harry. I wasted it on Nelson. I had my little hand of cards and played them and now I'm folded, I'm through. My husband hates me and I hate him and we don't even have any money to split up! I'm scared—*so* scared. And my kids are scared, too. I'm trash and they're trash and they know it." (312)

She has bet everything on Nelson and lost, but Harry reassures her, thinking to himself (but not saying aloud to Pru) that no one is trash, that God lifts people up and makes them into angels. In an excess of emotion, Rabbit pulls his daughter-in-law closer, moves her hand on to him, and kisses her.

Rain whips at the screen. The leak onto the windowsill accelerates its tapping. A brilliant close flash shocks the air everywhere and less than a second later a heart-stopping crack and splintering of thunder crushes the house from above. As if in overflow of this natural heedlessness, Pru says, "Shit," jumps from the bed, slams shut the window, pulls down the shade, tears open her bathrobe and sheds it, and, reaching down, pulls her nightie up over her head. Her tall pale wide-hipped nakedness in the dimmed room is lovely much as those pear trees in blossom along that block in Brewer last month were lovely, all his it had seemed, a piece of Paradise blundered upon, incredible. (314)

Thus ends section 2 of *Rabbit at Rest*, with Updike having bestowed "lovely" Pru on Rabbit, though Rabbit's sense of having attained paradise is short-lived.

The last section of the novel begins on the day following Father's Day, on which Rabbit does not receive a card until his grandchildren arrive for a cookout, bearing ironic Gary Larsen cards they obviously did not pick out themselves. Rabbit again is in charge at Springer Motors. He worries about the ragged state of its landscaping and the wrappers that blow over from the new Pizza Hut that has replaced a previous takeout place, seemingly more concerned about the ragged yews than about his son. He has twice gone reluctantly to Philadelphia to participate in Nelson's rehab therapy. In Rabbit's mind "all this 'talking through' and 'processing' therapists like to do cheapens the world's facts; it reduces decisions that were the best people could do at the time to dream moves, to reflexes that have been 'processed' in a million previous cases like so much shredded wheat. He feels anticipated and discounted in advance, whatever he says, and increasingly aggravated, and winds up telling Janice and Pru to go next time without him." (316)

The cars sell themselves. Rabbit echoes the Toyota slogan of the time, "Who could ask for anything more?" a question with thematic implications in Updike's novel, also. What is left to Rabbit? What else is there for him to do, where else is there for him to go now that he is back to the same job he was doing a decade before? He keeps young sales reps Benny and Elvira on the sales floor for their local connections and ability to deal with younger buyers but wonders if they were involved with Nelson in the looting of the dealership, and he feels a generational difference from them. Even the impending breakup of the Soviet empire is not reassuring to him but worrisome, a change in a world that had come to seem familiar. "'It's like nobody's in charge of the other side anymore. I miss it,' he says. 'The cold war. It gave you a reason to get up in the morning'" (320). Benny and Elvira do not respond or take the bait when Rabbit tries to roil the waters by bringing up abortion, though Benny is a Roman Catholic and Elvira pro-choice. Rabbit seems to have become irrelevant.

Meanwhile outside accountants are sorting through the dealership's financial records, and they discover that a man named Owen Barfield bought a new Toyota each month from December through April. Rabbit remembers Barfield, a gay psychologist nicknamed "Slim" whom Nelson partied with, with a secure government job training high school dropouts. Actually he has been dead since December, but he is still alive in the computer systems at the local bank, which monthly extends him a new loan check that is cashed but never logged into the dealership's accounts, instead going into another account set up somewhere by Lyle or Nelson. Rabbit asks the head accountant why common sense failed to put a stop to this and learns that "common sense has gone out the window. . . . the computer checked his credit and liked it and the loan was approved" (326). The loss to the dealership from this scam alone is about two hundred thousand dollars. Meanwhile the paradise that was Rabbit's evening in bed with Pru has soured as well, "as if it had never been. He and Pru are severely polite with each other, and Janice . . . has ceased to create many occasions when the households mingle" (327–28).

Less than a month later, Rabbit gets his own parade, and a far more triumphal one than the Columbus Day parade he dodged in *Rabbit Redux*. In a great set-piece description, a recuperated Rabbit leads the Mount Judge Fourth of July parade in costume as Uncle Sam, even though he now lives on the other side of Brewer rather than in Mount Judge. He gets the role partly because he is tall and partly because the organizing committee members remember him from his high school basketball days of glory but mostly because his granddaughter Judy has suggested him to the parade committee members, who also happen to be leaders of her Girl Scout troop.

Rabbit "has become more corpulent than our national symbol," perhaps reflecting the state of the United States in 1989, but the Uncle Sam costume conceals his belly if he leaves the striped trousers unbuttoned to accommodate it (328). As they fuss over preparations, Janice suggests that the accompanying wig makes him look "like a very big red-faced woman. . . . I never saw your female side before. I bet you would have made a nicer woman than either your mother or Mim." Rabbit finds this insulting, but Janice insists it instead is "interesting," and they omit the wig, which makes Uncle Sam's top hat unsteady. The fake goatee slims his face, in Janice's view, and she wonders why Rabbit never grew a beard in a "subtle past tense that keeps creeping into her remarks about him" (329), an ominous foreboding of where the novel is leading.

The staging area for the parade is on the grounds of Rabbit's old high school, now a junior high and soon to be torn down because of its pervasive asbestos contamination and the fire risk posed by its wooden floors. Still it is familiar, reassuring ground, the sort of place where Rabbit can show at his best. Reminiscing again, he expects to see his old girlfriend Mary Ann there in "saddle shoes and white socks and a short pleated cheerleader's skirt. . . . Instead, strange people with puzzled Eighties faces keep asking directions, because he is dressed as Uncle Sam and should know. He has to tell them he doesn't know anything" (330). He sends Judy off to try to buy double-faced Scotch tape to secure his precariously attached goatee, but she can find only the single-sided version, and Harry is sent to the head of the parade, preceded only by a rapidly distancing patrol car, to follow a parade route that he remembers from childhood. He is first greeted as Uncle Sam but then more and more recognized by his old nickname from his high school basketball glory days and cheered as "Rabbit . . . hotshot!" Even his improvisation, Scotch taping the goatee to his chin, draws cheers from a crowd notably younger—and barer in dress—than he remembers from his past. "A spirit of indulgence, a conspiring to be amused, surrounds and upholds his parade as he leads it down the stunning emptiness at the center of the familiar slanting streets" (335).

The parade vehicles play recorded music of World War II, big band icon Glenn Miller's version of "American Patrol" and Kate Smith's "God Bless America" (from the same era), interspersed with the Beatles' "Yesterday" and "Imagine." So far as Rabbit can tell, the whole town "still loves him, as it did when he would score forty-two points for them in a single home game. . . . Harry's eyes burn and the impression giddily—as if he has been lifted up to survey all human history—grows upon him, making his heart thump worse and worse, that all in all this is the happiest fucking country the world has ever seen" (336–37).

The parade is a high point of the novel, and perhaps the high point of Rabbit's public life after high school, but it is followed by the death of Thelma. She dies at the end of July, at age fifty-five. Her kind personality had been warped by "hallucinations, raving sarcastic anger"; her death occurs in the same week as an air disaster that illustrates the random quality of death and survival. The news reports describe the plane's "breaking up in a giant fireball, and yet over a hundred surviving, some of them dangling upside down from the seat belts in a section of the fuselage, some of them walking away and getting lost in the cornfields next to the runway" (337). The lost quality fits Rabbit as well.

Rabbit might once have been able to share his parade triumph with Thelma, but instead goes with Janice to Thelma's funeral, stopping at a local Cineplex to ask the way to the Harrisons' "no-brand-name church." The theater is showing *Honey, I Shrunk the Kids; Batman; Ghostbusters II; Karate Kid III; Dead Poets Society;* and *Great Balls of Fire,* the biography of 1950s pioneering rock 'n' roll icon Jerry Lee Lewis. No one at the Cineplex can offer directions to the place of worship, and when Rabbit and Janice finally arrive at the "warehouse with windows" that is the church, its brown-suited pastor looks "like the plump young manager of an appliance store" and offers a homily that reveals he knows nothing essential about Thelma. Rather he describes a generic, saintly sufferer he met in a hospital, offering "rote assurances, the psalm about green pastures, the verses from Ecclesiastes about a time for everything, the hymn that says now the day is over" (338–39). The entire service is banal in the extreme, revealing nothing essential of the woman who had loved Rabbit.

Outside after the service, Rabbit discovers that Webb Murkett, now in his sixties, has replaced once-nubile Cindy with a new wife in her twenties and that Cindy has let herself go to "the standard Diamond County female build— bosom like a shelf and ass like you're carrying your own bench around with you. . . . He had wanted Cindy and wound up with Thelma. Now both are beyond desiring" (340). Cindy would "sink any Sunfish you'd try to sail with her now" (341), he uncharitably thinks, though he takes a moment to interact with her, still a limited person, whose main concern seems to be the state of her alimony and the fact that any money she earns from her dead-end job is subtracted from it.

Thelma's three sons are men now, while Rabbit's son is not present; instead Nelson is living in a halfway house after treatment for his cocaine addiction. Ronnie Harrison wants to fight Rabbit over his affair with Thelma, whom he says Rabbit did not love. Ronnie tells him that Thelma had wasted herself on him and then asked Ronnie's forgiveness. To this the ever-competitive Rabbit has no graceful response, rather the opposite: "'Ronnie,' he whispers. 'I did appreciate her. I did. She was a fantastic lay'" (344). As they rejoin their kin in front of the onlookers, all of whom seem to have intuited the subject of their argument, Ronnie and Rabbit execute a perfect crisscross as if they were still on the basketball court decades before, still teammates. The old memory still rules them. They remain linked. Rabbit absolves himself of any guilt feelings: since Ronnie "once screwed Ruth a whole weekend in Atlantic City and then bragged to him about it, [Rabbit] can't feel sorry for him at all" (345).

Natsume Shimada of Toyota's national sales headquarters arrives at the dealership at summer's end to deliver the final word on the embezzlement, a week before Nelson is scheduled to return from rehab. Rabbit wears a new suit of gray metallic fabric "developed . . . while doing the moon shots" as he greets Shimada (346). Their polite conversation ranges from tennis to Toyota's efforts at affirmative action for black Americans (notably lacking at Springer Motors) to Japan's efforts to follow the model of the postwar United States with the clear implication that Japan now finally has bested its rival. Throughout Shimada makes reference to Americans' lack of discipline, citing the dog excrement he sees on the streets of Torrance, California, as his major example.

Shimada then lays the situation on the line to Rabbit: Springer Motors owes $145,800 to Toyota. If the debt is repaid by the end of August, Shimada promises no criminal prosecution, but even so the Toyota franchise agreement and the gravy train it brought to Springer Motors will be ended. All the new Toyotas will be transferred to a nearby dealership owned by former Springer employee Rudy Krauss. Shimada asks for Elvira's business card as he leaves, obviously intending that she will move along with the vehicles.

Nelson returns from rehab and immediately is reinstated at Springer Motors by Janice, even though its franchise agreement with Toyota by now has been canceled. She seems more engaged by her nascent career in real estate than by the difficulties of the dealership. When Rabbit objects to the return, calling Nelson a loser, both Janice and Pru claim he is being unfair. Janice opines that "he's a new person. We can't deny him a chance," and Pru echoes, "He really has changed, Harry" (369). Meanwhile Nelson coasts along with hardly reassuring references to his twelve-step program and its obligatory "higher power": "Such knowingness, such induced calm and steadiness and virtue; it makes Rabbit feel claustrophobic" (370). Judy is happy to have her father back, however. After Janice cuts Rabbit loose from his responsibilities at the dealership, citing concern for his declining health, Nelson unrealistically proposes transforming Springer Motors into a halfway house. To his father this proposal is the clearest possible example of how little Nelson understands the world at this point and of how self-centered he still is.

Rabbit's temporary refuge from his demotion is a round of golf with Ronnie Harrison, his old buddy and enemy, who is playing as his guest. Ronnie has had to resign from the country club because of Thelma's final medical bills. He has become "a widower, with the face of a bleached prune, pulled-looking wrinkles down from his eyes, an old guy's skin showing pink at the cheekbones. Harry feels that Ronnie has always been with him, a presence he couldn't avoid, an aspect of himself he didn't want to face but now does. That clublike cock, those slimy jokes . . . what the hell, we're all just human, bodies with brains at one end and the rest just plumbing" (372).

As they play they carefully try to avoid any mention of Thelma after their mutual explosion at her funeral. First Rabbit talks expansively of current events, including the Voyager space probe's flight past Neptune, as he hits several excellent shots and seems certain to win their game, and then Ronnie takes up the space probe as a subject as Rabbit muffs a couple of shots, tries too hard, and loses the match. Rabbit thinks apropos of Voyager and much more, "How can you believe how much void there is?" This characteristic concern of his leads to the unavoidable subject of Thelma. He asks Ronnie, "Do you miss her?"

Ronnie gives him an angle squint. His eyelids look sore under his white eyelashes. "Do you?"

Ambushed, Rabbit can barely pretend he does. He used Thelma, and then she used up. "Sure," he says.

Ronnie clears his ropy throat and checks that the zipper on his bag is up and then shoulders the bag to take to his car. "Sure you do," he says. "Try to sound sincere. You never gave a fuck. No. Excuse me. A fuck is exactly what you gave."

Harry hangs between impossible alternatives—again to tell Ronnie how much he enjoyed going to bed with Thelma (with Ronnie's smiling photo watching from atop the Harrisons' dresser) or to claim that he didn't. He answers merely, "Thelma was a lovely woman." (375)

Rabbit attempts to avoid conflict, as is usual for him, but as Ronnie says, the bottom of his world has dropped out. He passes on Rabbit's invitation to have a beer at the club after the game. Their relationship is over. They will not play golf together again, if only because the country club's rules forbid continuing guests. The rule seems a relief to both men.

Nelson meets his father at the Penn Park house after Rabbit's unsatisfactory golf match, and he has an alternative suggestion for Rabbit regarding the dealership, a far cannier one than his previous harebrained halfway house scheme. His great idea of the night before is that Springer Motors continue its highly successful used car sales but also sell Yamaha Wave Runners, motorcycles, and snowmobiles and trailers for all three. Enthused, Nelson has already discussed the idea with Yamaha's national sales office and has gotten Janice's approval for presenting it to Rabbit. Still smarting from his loss to Ronnie, Rabbit finds this "the dumbest thing I've ever heard. Jet skis are a fad. Next year it'll be jet roller skates. The profit on a toy like a motorcycle or a snowmobile is maybe a tenth that on a solid family car. . . . there's a Depression coming," he concludes in a final expression of pessimism about the scheme's prospects (378). Rabbit's shortsightedness suggests that it really is a new day and that Nelson indeed may understand this world as Rabbit no longer does. Nelson now may be equipped to make a success out of the business that he previously ran into the ground.

A further blow to Rabbit's morale is not long in coming. Janice proposes selling their comfortable Penn Park burrow for the last decade as the first transaction of her new real estate career and moving back in to the old Springer family home at 89 Joseph Street to live with Nelson's family. This proposal does not turn out so well, however, when in a spirit of excessive truthfulness Pru reveals to Janice and Nelson that she slept with Rabbit. (In Janice's view Pru is perhaps trying to stave off too much multigenerational family togetherness on Joseph Street.)

In a phone call summoning him from Franklin Place to a family meeting on Joseph Street, Janice characterizes Rabbit's sleeping with Pru as hurtful and inconsiderate beyond anything he has done before. Rabbit "can picture Janice's face exactly, twisted and helpless and ugly, old age collapsing in upon her." He knows her too well and can hear too much of a past script here, Janice "saying standard things, and into the vault of his shocked and shamed consciousness there is admitted a whiff of boredom." Janice pronounces Rabbit's dalliance with Pru as "the worst thing you've done, ever, ever" and tells him that she will never forgive him (393). The clichés build in response to his ham-handed attempts to diffuse her anger with jokes, culminating in psychobabble as Janice reports that Nelson "is being very calm and using all that good psychological work they did at the treatment center. He says this will need a lot of processing and we must begin right now. If we don't start right in we'll all harden in our positions" (394). Rabbit cannot get Janice to tell him how Nelson actually feels; indeed, she likely does not know.

Ordered by Janice to come and "for once" undo the consequences of his actions, "Rabbit sees clearly what to do" (395). Instead of going to a showdown on Joseph Street, he packs a couple of bags and runs again—toward Florida by car, pretty much reprising his flight at the end of *Rabbit, Run* though with the advantage that his thirty years of Florida trips have clued him in to the fastest routes to take, whether by night or by day.

While staying at a Ramada Inn in Georgia on September 1, 1989, the second night of his trip south, Rabbit learns of baseball commissioner Bart Giamatti's fatal heart attack at age fifty-one, which prefigures Rabbit's own heart attack at novel's end. Rabbit reaches the Florida condo in time for Labor Day, goes golfing, and waits for his phone to be installed, hoping that Janice will call. He walks for his health and tries to cut down on bad foods. Meanwhile Hurricane Hugo is heading for Florida. The storm proves anticlimactic for Rabbit, however, since it mostly misses Florida and instead heavily impacts the Carolinas.

Rabbit comes upon a pickup ball game in progress and ends up playing one-on-one basketball with a black kid, nicknamed Tiger, and has another heart attack. He ends up winning the game—or thinks he does—and tries to tell Janice this on his deathbed when she arrives at the hospital. He also tries (it is unclear whether he succeeds) to tell Nelson of his half-sister, Annabelle. "It isn't so bad," he concludes as he dies at age fifty-six, on the day of Nelson's tenth wedding anniversary.

Rabbit Remembered

Rabbit's continuing influence on the lives of those who knew and loved him is the subject matter of the novella *Rabbit Remembered*, which was published along with twelve short stories in the collection *Licks of Love*. Having killed off Rabbit in *Rabbit at Rest*, Updike focused on those left behind to continue the exploration and criticism of American life that had been his aim at least since *Rabbit Redux* and to provide readers more information about the other characters of the tetralogy.

Rabbit Remembered opens with a tour de force of point of view, focusing on Janice, now Janice Harrison. She is sixty-two and remarried to Ronnie Harrison, Rabbit's sometime friend and great rival Ronnie, though the passage makes her seem older than her chronological age, elderly and emotionally fragile, as the preceding novel had suggested she was becoming. She opens the front door of the house on Joseph Street to find Annabelle Byer standing there, looking vaguely familiar and unsettling. (Annabelle's resemblance to Rabbit is initially unrecognized but evokes memories of him in several characters). Apparently Janice had not known of her. At first she thinks Annabelle might be a salesperson or a Jehovah's Witness, or maybe a beggar, despite her respectable appearance, "but the something pleasant and kind and calm about the girl, who is these as well as troubled and trembling, holds the door open" (180). Annabelle is thirty-nine, a licensed practical nurse, unmarried, and facing the aftermath of the death of her mother; it was Ruth's wish that she pursue the Angstrom family connection. Janice is clearly uncomfortable in the situation, and the most masterful element in the entire description of her day is the way in which Updike conveys her discomfort and the limitations of her sympathy for others: "'Why?' Janice cries, fighting back a pressure. 'Why not let the past lie? Why stir up what can't be helped?'"(190). Annabelle sympathizes with her, though in fact the older woman comes across as quite selfish, and leaves, but the rest of Janice's day is marked by her working to come to terms with this new intrusion of the memory of Rabbit into her life. She worries about a couple who would not consider making an offer on a house she was trying to sell, repeatedly misses bids in her bridge game with three friends, and when Ronnie comes home tries to engage him in a discussion of what she has learned. She has been thrown off center.

That Janice wishes to avoid the past is also ironic in that Annabelle's appearance immediately leads her to remember the past in great detail. The first thing that she notices after the younger woman's declaration of identity is a passing white mail truck with blue and red stripe, and in a moment of great subtlety on Updike's part, Janice immediately remembers that mail trucks used to be green and "mailmen used to be men; now theirs is a mail-lady" (181). She is thrown back into her past in multiple memories, and the reader is cued in to Updike's nostalgic take on life in Pennsylvania as it has developed over the years.

Janice is not an important enough or complex enough character to carry the entire novella, however, and Updike rapidly transitions to more promising ground, making Annabelle's appearance the means to an exploration of her half-brother, Nelson, who is still living with his mother and stepfather in the house on Joseph Street. Pru and their two children now have left him for life in Pru's hometown, Akron, Ohio. For most readers Nelson has likely been an annoying presence throughout much of the tetralogy, a young man who cannot connect to or understand his father and who never has experienced anything comparable to the transitory moments of excellence on the basketball court that served Rabbit as touchstones throughout his life.

Nelson has been a consistent, self-sabotaging loser, and now at age forty-two he works in a low-paying job as a counselor at Fresh Start, a local halfway house for the mentally ill. Here, however, he seems to have found his own level. "He has learned his limits" (227)—he does not wish to earn a more advanced degree or work in a supervisory position—but the phrases he uses to lead group and individual therapy sessions seem to have moved him beyond rote recitation into something closer to actual empathy with his clients. If he is not an excellent counselor, he is at least competent and cares about his clients, and he carries these qualities into his own life. At some moments he shines, as when he correctly reads the truths and misstatements of a borderline schizophrenic young man, Michael DiLorenzo, who had become ill at college after a previously golden life. Nelson gives the young man pragmatic advice and then explains the situation to Michael's parents. The DiLorenzos are shattered by what has happened to their son. The father has built a successful dry cleaning business that he has hoped his son would run after college, and sees his own dream laid waste. The mother thinks the son's life has gone "down the drain into craziness." Nelson's own difficult life has equipped him well to speak on relationships between parents and children, however: "He's still the child you raised, the child you love. He's still Michael. He's just fallen ill, and needs you more than most young men need their parents" (238). Nelson is empathetic, but he also has moved on: "These dysfunctionals make him aware of how functional he is" (239).

In a technique Updike uses elsewhere, the context for the later sections of the novella is formed by important events shared by many people. Echoing Updike's use of Hurricane Hugo in Rabbit at Rest, in Rabbit Remembered Hurricane Floyd, which struck the United States in mid-September 1999, forms the background to the interview with the young schizophrenic and his parents and to Nelson's first meeting with Annabelle over lunch, foreshadowing changes in all these lives. A disastrous Thanksgiving dinner in which he attempts to bring Annabelle into the family circle will lead Nelson to make his own break with his mother and her new husband, and events of Christmas and New Year's Eve 1999 further push Nelson out of his comfort zone and help to establish new directions for him and for Annabelle.

Making the relationship between Annabelle and Nelson the focus of most of the novella is narratively brilliant in that in the guise of telling Annabelle what her father was like, Nelson (and Updike) are able credibly to revisit many of the events and themes of the earlier novels. Most are new to Annabelle, if not to faithful readers, as are Nelson's newly mature judgments of his father.

A Note on Nelson and Generations

Nelson is forty-two years old in the present time of *Rabbit Remembered*, and thus he would have been born in about 1958, conventionally making him a late member of the post–World War II "Baby Boom" generation. The Baby Boom is generally considered to extend roughly 1946–64 and is identified with a considerable uptick in birth rates that resulted from 1950s affluence and the end of the war. Members of this relatively large generation have been highly influential in American culture. They are noted for their relative affluence, high expectations, moralistic self-confidence, and the "generation gap," an adversarial relationship with their parents' more traditional values. Nelson's antipathy for his father and mother seen in the earlier novels fits this pattern well, particularly his rejection of Rabbit's material success and complacent values. This reaction is tempered, and his father is seen more positively by Nelson by the time of *Rabbit Remembered* as he thinks back upon some of their happiest moments together, as father drove son to one activity or another: "as [Rabbit] got older and tame he radiated happiness at just the simplest American things, driving along in an automobile, the radio giving off music, the heater giving off heat, delivering his son somewhere in this urban area that he knew block by block, intersection by intersection" (252).

As a late Boomer, Nelson's many dissatisfactions also fit the pattern of another generational model, named in 2007 by author Jonathan Pontell: "Generation Jones." Pontell's Generation Jones extends perhaps from 1954 to 1965 and overlaps with the late Baby Boomers and the early members of so-called Generation X (born roughly between 1961 and 1981 and popularized in the Canadian Douglas Coupland's 1991 novel, *Generation X: Tales for an Accelerated Culture*). The salient point about Generation Jones relevant to Nelson is that its members were born into and brought up in the optimistic milieu of the 1950s and early 1960s but came to maturity and entered the workforce in a more economically difficult and morally ambiguous time. Widespread U.S. deindustrialization and the aftermath of Vietnam and the sexual revolution shaped this group's world in a way not characteristic of their older siblings of the early Baby Boom. Thus Nelson's highly unattractive complaining and general inability to fit into the world are not merely a matter of personal characterization or idiosyncrasy but are also generational, representing his age cohort and time and rendering his characterization a part of Updike's continuing attempt to draw a portrait of his own time and place in American history and culture. Updike had chronicled the pattern before Pontell named and described it.

Nelson's lunch with Annabelle almost immediately follows his sessions with the dysfunctional DiLorenzos. It takes place in the same uncertain context of the hurricane's coming inland. "Is this a hurricane or not?" is the question of the day as Nelson walks to his meeting—and by implication the question regarding bringing Annabelle into the family. Will her introduction cause a disaster, or will it not amount to much? Along the way the streets are less populated but not entirely deserted, some people going about their usual activities: "The weather is being snubbed. People are in rebellion at having it hyped on TV so relentlessly, to bring up ratings" (242–43). The siblings meet at the Greenery, a health food restaurant that has succeeded several previous establishments in its location, reaching back in time to Rabbit's youth in the city. The restaurant already is changing again, adding less healthful menu options in response to the actual tastes of its clientele.

Unsure of how the lunch will go, Nelson reverts to earlier habits, being cynical to Annabelle about their roles as caregivers, but she calls him on this pose on the basis of her experiences in private nursing with the elderly: "You don't mean that. In the abstract you can feel that way, but not when you're face to face with the patient. . . . Even at the end there's something in there, a soul or whatever, you have to love" (247). The application to Rabbit is not directly stated by Updike but probably clear to most readers, as is the reminder of the author's concern with religious questions and with mortality.

Nelson goes on to relate memories of his father and decides Rabbit was better than he gave him credit for. Annabelle tells her own story of her meeting Rabbit roughly two decades before at the car dealership (a scene depicted in *Rabbit Is Rich*), and the hurricane finally has a measurable effect: the electricity goes out. Their aging waitress misidentifies the two of them as lovebirds, and they have dessert, crumb cake in the half light—decidedly not a health food item. Despite the fact that he has been eating there once or twice a week, Nelson notices for the first time a couple of children in the mural on the wall, "a boy and a girl wearing old-fashioned German outfits, pigtails and lederhosen, holding hands, lost" (255). The point is clear: he and Annabelle are like Hansel and Gretel in the forest, still lost children, looking to resolve their relationships with their father. Nelson "hungers for a hurricane, he realizes—for an upheaval tearing everything loose" (257).

The upheaval occurs over Thanksgiving, America's traditional festival of family togetherness. Janice remains decidedly against Annabelle as Nelson suggests somehow inviting her into the family. Janice's limitations of imagination and empathy are again clear as she complains, "What am I supposed to say—this is my dead husband's bastard daughter from forty years ago? It was humiliating enough at the time, that whole nightmare" (259). But Nelson is insistent, proposing a dinner including his stepbrothers (Ronnie's sons) and their families. Janice hits on Thanksgiving as the appropriate dinner occasion. She hopes it will be an occasion on which Annabelle may get lost in the crowd. "Poor Nelson," she thinks. "He has this bee in his bonnet—doing something for this girl nobody knows. It clutches at Janice's heart, to think that he always

wanted more of a family than they could give him—a bigger, happier one. . . .
The boy had wanted her and Harry's happiness so. . . . And all this healing he
still wants for everybody, it makes her heart gripe to think of how they must
have hurt him" (261).

Thanksgiving dinner proves not auspicious, with a guest list of thirteen including Ronnie's three sons and their families and the elderly Dietrichs, descendants of the owners of one of the city's now-defunct textile mills, still supported
by their investments into the third generation. None of Ronnie's sons are
entirely successful. One is a university dropout now supporting a family as a
carpenter "nailing two-by-fours into tacky house frames"; another an aging
gay dancer in New York City who now works for a ticket agency, selling admis-
sions to the shows in which he once had hoped to perform; the third and most
successful is a computer programmer, "though since it was a field where the
brightest and luckiest made millions before thirty perhaps he felt like a failure"
(285). All know of Rabbit's affair with their mother, resent it, and subtly have
it in for Nelson as his heir.

Dinner goes reasonably well until a fourth bottle of wine has been con-
sumed, and then the conversation turns right-wing and political, against for-
eigners, blacks, and President Bill Clinton and his wife, Hillary, and particularly
against her then-bruited campaign for the U.S. Senate representing New York
state. Nelson defends the Clintons, and Annabelle realizes "she loves Clinton
. . . from all those hours at the television set, letting his A-student earnestness
wash over her, his lip-biting pauses for the judicious word, his gently raspy
hillbilly accent. . . . her President had kept doing his job with the entire country full of cheap and ugly cracks" (295–96). Ronnie drunkenly focuses on the
Monica Lewinsky scandal and castigates "Slick Willie" for bringing the phrase
"blow job" out into public debate. Richard Nixon, Ronald Reagan, and the fall
of Communism are quickly mixed into the toxic conversation, and Janice, also
drunk, "tries to focus. She had been thinking of how much like Harry Nelson
was, defending Presidents. Her son has that expression on his face Harry used
to call 'white around the gills.' Why do they do it, care so much about those
distant men? They identify" (298).

Janice attempts to break the toxic pattern by clearing the table and inviting Annabelle to help her and thus drawing her away from the argument, but
instead almost all the attendees end up crammed into the kitchen. Ronnie is
conscious of Annabelle's sexual appeal and verbally assaults her as they load
the dishwasher: "A blow job's just a way of showing affection. . . . You're your
mother's daughter, all right. . . . I knew your mother once. Before she got involved with that jerk Angstrom. . . . She'd fuck anybody. . . . It must feel funny
. . . being the illegitimate daughter of a hooer and a bum" (299–301). In a final

piece of self-righteous cruelty Ronnie compares Annabelle to her mother and makes reference to Annebelle's hair—and pubic hair: "Now I know. Looks just like her, without the ginger in her hair. And cunt, my guess is" (301).

As he had with the DiLorenzos at the halfway house, Nelson rises again to an occasion, making a gesture equal to the situation as he tells Ronnie that "every time you went up against [his father], he beat you out. You, you're a loser" (301). He tells Janice that he is leaving for good, saying remarkably gracious goodbyes to the Dietrichs and others who had remained in the dining room and even neatly tearing off a length of paper towel before leaving the kitchen so that humiliated Annabelle can dry her hands as she says her goodbyes, "her throat sore from her choked-down sobs" (302). His last impression of the house is of the front porch that he had loved as he remembers the odor of its now-vanished wicker armchair and cushioned glider. "His senses feel clean again, the rain sharp on his face, the patter in the maple leaves overhead distinct, each drop, as he tugs his sister toward the tired white Corolla he brought her in. The house across the street . . . is dark, empty. They neighbors are away for the holiday, and thus miss seeing the heir leave 89 Joseph Street for good" (303). It is a bravura scene on Updike's part, and the change for Nelson is equal to nothing that came before in his life. Like his father did repeatedly many years before, Nelson is running, but this time it is the absolutely right thing to do.

Updike takes readers through Nelson's move into a furnished room near downtown, his developing relationship with Annabelle, and even some backsliding in his break with Ronnie and Janice. Apparently he has become a person who tries to put things together, however much of his earlier life was spent in breaking them apart. He arranges for Pru and their son, Roy, to visit for the holidays, after Christmas, though their daughter, Judy, now almost twenty, will stay in Akron with a well-off boyfriend. Emails to Roy inserted into the text advance the plot expeditiously during the month between the November and December holidays and allow readers to see Nelson trying out the role of father, one in which he previously has had little success. As with his counseling, he is not a star in this role, but he is competent, if a little behind the times in computer literacy and the latest teen slang. Nelson again comes across as a caring person, and he faces some of his failings, notably his earlier lapse in not leaving the Joseph Street house to build an independent marriage when Pru suggested it. His current pay of eighty-five dollars a week rent plus child support has left him strapped. He lets Roy know about his "half-aunt," Annabelle, and apologizes fairly gracefully for having missed Roy's birthday. Nelson is not the perfect father, but he is improving.

He also somewhat slyly passes along his new phone number in one of the emails to Roy and thus is not surprised when a week later his wife calls to discuss arrangements for the visit and the status of their children. Roy is spending much of his time on his computer, and Judy is thinking of becoming a flight attendant. Nelson is more insistent about knowing what is going on, including asking about Pru's romantic life, a topic he realizes he would not have raised a week before when he still lived on Joseph Street. Their difference in age (Pru is a year older) had been a source of embarrassment throughout their relationship out of proportion to its actual significance, and now "in recent years the year's difference had swung back to mattering less, a slightly awkward fact like her being left-handed."

"My life with you is too small!" had been Pru's past complaint to Nelson, but now she is looking to find something beyond her current job as a lawyer's secretary and has given notice to her employer. Nelson suppresses some negative thoughts about her desire to avoid a routine life—he now knows how much routine is involved in most lives—and blandly suggests, "It doesn't sound as if the job uses all your abilities" (312–13). Again this is not a stellar response but a competent one, reflecting Nelson's growth into manhood in his forties as well as his ability to bring his counseling skills to bear in everyday situations.

Nelson spends most of Christmas Day alone, having exchanged mostly unsatisfactory gifts with Ronnie and Janice early in the day (Ronnie's gift of a book by the Dalai Lama leads Nelson to compare Rabbit's serene air of repose to that of the religious leader). Nelson leaves the house on Joseph Street before Ronnie's children arrive. Back at his apartment, he eats a frozen dinner and watches the Oahu Bowl—and deals with the news that his young patient Michael DiLorenzo killed himself on Christmas Eve, suffocating himself with a transparent bag from his father's dry cleaning business. Annabelle is in Las Vegas with a girlfriend and has looked up Nelson's Aunt Mim, though earlier she had attempted to beg off doing so during another of their lunches at the Greenery on the grounds that "it'll be one more thing" (321).

In the preceding weeks, Nelson also has been lunching with his boyhood friend Billy Fosnacht, now a successful dental implant surgeon but a two-time loser at marriage. They meet at a former chophouse now become a healthier pasta restaurant, on December 15, 1999, the day after cartoonist Charles M. Schulz announced he was ending the comic strip *Peanuts,* drawing an end to another touchstone of American life in the second half of the twentieth century. Over pasta bowties with diced shrimp and mushroom ravioli, Billy is soon telling Nelson of his insistently recurring dreams of death, and Nelson realizes that Billy is there paying for lunch and Pellegrino water in return for free therapy. He is not pleased and hard-heartedly suggests that death is like a nap without waking up, but he also realizes "there is agony here, even if Billy is a comical old friend" (325).

Nelson suggests a double date for New Year's Eve, which will be the beginning of a new millennium and the end to Updike's century. It will be Nelson and Pru, Billy and Annabelle, for dinner at a club overlooking the city and a movie (*American Beauty*, the story of a discontented American husband), followed by the New Year's celebrations back in Brewer. Annabelle is skeptical about his idea:

> She doesn't say yes or no. She says, "They say there may be terrorist attacks."
>
> "In Brewer? On what, the pretzel factories?"
>
> "The mayor of Seattle cancelled their celebration today."
>
> "He has the Space Needle to worry about."
>
> "Nelson, I hope you know what you're doing." This is Annabelle's way of agreeing.
>
> "No," he says, feeling cheerful for the first time this terminal week, "I don't, frankly." (337)

They have a pleasant dinner, somewhat marred by their rushing to make their reservation time. After the movie, though, Nelson turns the wrong way exiting the theater parking lot and sends them away from Brewer and the midnight celebrations. This is sorted out, though tensions are high, and Nelson resents Pru's detailed instructions delivered "in a low, sharply aimed wife's voice" (345) on to how to change directions by exiting the freeway and crossing the overpass. Billy is in the back seat with Annabelle recounting another of his nightmares of death, and while Annabelle deals "silkily" with his anxieties, Nelson somehow manages to break in to the conversation with a seemingly out of the blue but therapeutic question, asking how far Annabelle's stepfather went with his affection and evoking her confession that she indeed had been molested by the man, had not known what to do, and had blamed herself and been relieved when he died. This is a scene of high drama and risk, and several times during it Nelson has "the sensation of a fifth person in the car" (345): Rabbit.

As they drive Nelson "knows where he is now," and they pass the tawdry side of Brewer. They can see "the silhouette of Mt. Judge far to their right, crowned by the distant lights of the Pinnacle Hotel, where they had been, the four of them, sitting and eating and making polite conversation, a few hours ago. Time does wonders." Pru comforts Annabelle: "So you got pawed. So did I. My father was a crumb-bum, when you think of it. It's not the end of the world." Nelson remembers something Pru told him when she was new to his family: "*Why, honey. I think from what I've seen your parents are quite fond of each other. Couples that have stayed together that long, they must have something*" (348, Updike's emphasis). He and Pru have been married about two decades.

They drive past the abandoned building of the old Springer Motors Toyota Agency. "By inner moonlight Nelson sees the ghosts of his father and himself and Charlie Stavros and Elvira Ollenbach standing at the boarded-up windows looking out at Route 111 for customers that will never come." Annabelle recalls her meeting with Rabbit there, years before, and Pru contributes the information that Nelson "lost the agency up his nose" to his cocaine addiction. Nelson complains at the revelation.

> "Siblings should have no secrets," Pru says, and makes he knows without looking, that prudish little mouth of hers, as if sucking on something tart. "Nelson wasn't always such a saint."
>
> "He was a pill of a sissy, in fact," Billy contributes, making the fun rougher. "A real little mamma's boy, terrified of his father, who was a pretty nice guy, actually." (350)

They pass into downtown Brewer, elegiacally described as it has changed over the years, Annabelle and Billy snuggling in the back seat, and Nelson faces one last trial. At the intersection where once stood Krolls department store (where Rabbit and Janice had met), the traffic light goes out at midnight. Annabelle suspects terrorists and begins to cry again while Billy feigns calm. "'Son of a bitch!' Nelson says. Decades of wrongs, hurts, unjust deaths press behind his eyes. . . . The city's fire alarms begin to wail, church bells are dully ringing" (351). And they are missing the fireworks. Cars are alternating at the dead light, and a large SUV tries to cut through out of turn, but Nelson will not back off, and his subcompact Corolla goes through the intersection in its proper turn. They feel that they have faced death and won, and Pru grants a reward: "I thought I'd stay at your place tonight" (353). Nelson has faced a monster in the guise of a Ford Expedition and triumphed. The moment may not be completely heroic, but it will do.

In the start of the new millennium, Nelson quits his job at the Fresh Start Center and moves to Akron to be with Pru and their children. In a sense this is a change that is not a change but an acknowledgement that Nelson has adult responsibilities. As he puts it to Annabelle in their telephone conversation that ends the novella, "Akron's a lot like Brewer except it's three times as big. It has the same river, and miles of row houses, and abandoned plants turned into something else . . . and no shortage of misery." He plans to look for a counseling job in drug rehab (unlike his previous clients, addicts not generally being suicidal), and he even remembers Annabelle's fortieth birthday, another sign of his maturation that contrasts with his earlier forgetting of Roy's birthday. He even finds an apt quotation from Ronnie's gift book: "The very motion of our life is toward happiness" (357).

When Annabelle announces her impending marriage to Billy, Nelson once again comes up with the appropriate response. In the weeks since Nelson's leaving Brewer, Billy has found Annabelle wonderful and she has reciprocated despite Billy's fears and inadequacies. In one of Updike's elegant stylistic formulations, "happiness for her is already rising in him, like water trembling upward" (358). When Annabelle asks Nelson to give her away at the wedding, he responds, "Gladly" (359).

These last developments risk being cloying or inadequate, but Updike handles them with assurance and control, perhaps more so than at other points in the tetralogy. Nelson is at rest, emotionally, and he has managed to find within himself something of the spirit that made his father an appealing if also sometimes appalling character. The reader is at rest also, content with the author's suggestion that lives have shape and meaning and that even out of chaos and miscommunication they may influence other lives for the better.

CHAPTER 3

The Maples Stories, Olinger Stories, and Other Short Fiction

The Maples Stories

The highly autobiographical Maples stories appeared over decades. Many of them were collected in *Museums and Women* (1972), *Too Far to Go* (1979), and *The Early Stories: 1953–1974* (2004), and all eighteen of them were compiled in *The Maples Stories* (2009). These stories are widely regarded as among Updike's greatest literary achievements, considered by some critics to be superior to his novels in portraying the changes in American culture and relationships from the 1950s into the mid-1970s. The final story, "Grandparenting," revisits the two main characters much later in life, long remarried but still bound together by their deepest link, their children, as their eldest daughter gives birth. The stories trace romance, marriage, parenthood, mutual disillusionment, and divorce and its aftermath of in the persons of Richard and Joan Maple, with the emphasis on their falling away from each other despite many points of sympathy between them and their mutual dedication to their four children. Readers who object to Rabbit and Janice Angstrom's many crass and insensitive features find in these stories a male and female protagonist who are much more in tune with their own emotions and capable of thinking critically about their individual and joint strengths and weaknesses. Even in divorce they value and sympathize with each other. As Updike put it in introducing the collection,

> Though the Maples stories trace the decline and fall of a marriage, they also illumine a history in many ways happy, of growing children and a million mundane moments shared. That a marriage ends is less than ideal; but all

things end under heaven, and if temporality is held to be invalidating, then nothing real succeeds. The moral of these stories is that all blessings are mixed. Also, that people are incorrigibly themselves. The musical pattern, the advance and retreat, of the Maples' duet is repeated over and over, ever more harshly transposed. They are shy, cheerful, and dissatisfied. They like each other and are mysteries to each other. One of them is usually feeling unwell, and the seesaw of their erotic interest rarely balances. Yet they talk, more easily than any other characters the author has acted as agent for. (*Maples Stories,* 11)

Here as elsewhere, Updike is an adept critic—even of his own work. These are appealing and human stories, and unlike the volumes of the Rabbit tetralogy, much more easily accessible to those who might be coming to his fiction for the first time.

Of the Maples stories, the sweet "Wife-Wooing," "Twin Beds in Rome," and "Separating" were often seen in college fiction anthologies during Updike's lifetime. The seesaw of erotic interest is at the center of "Wife-Wooing" (the second-published of the stories), which depicts Richard's frustration with Joan's seeming resistance to his advances and then her graceful agreement when he least expects it. The story could serve as a rejoinder to those critics who believe that Updike could neither write a credible female nor sympathize with her point of view.

"Twin Beds in Rome," the fourth story to be published, takes the couple on a spur-of-the-moment trip to the Eternal City in search of a way to live happily together and details the ways in which, as the Maples' status in life seems to advance, their relationship does not. Indeed Richard still sees his wife as "the secret woman he could never reach and at last wearied of trying to reach" (*Maples Stories* 56). Sleeping in twin beds at the hotel for the first time ever in their marriage, during the day they wander Rome from tourist attraction to tourist attraction. Dropping coins into the hands of one guide after another, his shoes pinching ominously until he buys a new pair of Italian loafers, Richard returns to their hotel room feeling ill and then wakes happy and cured. They now can tour in peace, "their marriage let go like an overgrown vine whose half-hidden stem has been slashed in the dawn by an ancient gardener. . . . She was happy, and, jealous of her happiness, he grew reluctant again to leave her" (64).

In "Separating" the Maples have the task of announcing their break to their four children, having waited until all are together at the beginning of summer. Their tennis court is barren after its first winter, both Richard and Joan long having observed "how often, among their friends, divorce followed a dramatic home improvement, as if the marriage were making one last effort to live"

(177). Joan has an orderly plan to announce the break to the children one after the other, from oldest (Judith, nineteen years old) to youngest, but as they have supper with three of the four, Richard's unstoppable tears lead to the revelation. Then he goes to the train station in the middle of the night to meet their fifteen-year-old son, Dickie, as he returns from a rock concert and has the conversation with him. He is brought up short by Dickie's question: "*Why*. It was a whistle of wind in a crack, a knife thrust, a window thrown open on emptiness. The waiting white face was gone, the darkness was featureless. Richard had forgotten why" (191).

In one of the final stories, "Gesturing," the now-divorced Maples go out together to have dinner and discuss their new significant others. In their conversation the cost of divorce and the impossibility of completely ending a relationship spanning half a lifetime become clear. The story's central image is of a windowpane in Richard's new apartment on which successive tenants have inscribed messages using the diamonds of engagement rings, including "With this ring/I thee wed." As their dinner concludes, Richard "saw through her words to what she was saying—that these lovers, however we love them, are not us, are not sacred as reality is sacred. We are reality. We have made children. We gave each other our young bodies. We promised to grow old together." Telling Richard a story about how the old plumber who worked on their once-shared house interrupted her in love-making with her new man, Joan makes a gesture that Richard thinks is "eager, shy, exquisite, diffident, trusting; he saw all its meanings and knew that she would never stop gesturing within him, never; though a decree come between them, even death, her gestures would endure, cut into glass" (*The Early Stories*, 808–9).

Olinger Stories: A Selection

Olinger Stories (1964), a collection of previously published short stories, includes such classics as "Pigeon Feathers" and seems somewhat modeled on earlier modernist collections such as Sherwood Anderson's *Winesburg, Ohio* (1919) and Ernest Hemingway's *In Our Time* (1925) in that the stories focus mostly on one young man. Unlike Anderson's George Willard and Hemingway's Nick Adams, Updike's young man is not a particular individual but a type; he always is centered somehow on fictional Olinger, more or less based on Updike's Shillington, Pennsylvania, and as he puts it in his introduction to the collection, "is always returning from hundreds of miles really."

Discussing these stories in the 1968 *Paris Review* interview, Updike explained something of why they may be so resonant for readers, as for him, and he also set himself in parallel with several great writers of the past. Usually diffident and self-effacing in interviews, here he suggests by comparison where he aimed his career: "I really don't think I'm alone among writers in caring about what they experienced in the first eighteen years of their life. Hemingway cherished the Michigan stories out of proportion, I would think, to their merit. Look at Twain. Look at Joyce. Nothing that happens to us after twenty is as free from self-consciousness because by then we have the vocation to write. Writers' lives break into two halves. At the point where you get your writerly vocation you diminish your receptivity to experience" (*Conversations* 28).

Thus *Olinger Stories* is a Künstlerroman (the story of the education of an artist), as are Anderson's, Hemingway's, and James Joyce's early works. The stories are written with the grace of much of the best of Updike's early work, a pure lyricism not always seen in his novels and other later works. All the stories appeared in the *New Yorker* beginning in 1954, with some also appearing in the story collections *The Same Door* (1959) and *Pigeon Feathers and Other Stories* (1962).

CHAPTER 4

Couples (1968)

Among the most successful of Updike's novels in terms of sales, with at least 4.2 million hardbound copies sold (Batchelor 29), *Couples* has been both praised and criticized for its depiction of the fictional Tarbox, Massachusetts, toward the end of the John F. Kennedy administration as a place of middle-class sexual experimentation and adultery. It led to Updike's first appearance on the cover of *Time,* on April 26, 1968, apparently over the objections of some of those in the newsmagazine's management as the novel's subject matter became obvious to them. The headline was "The Adulterous Society." Critic Diana Trilling in a review in the *Atlantic Monthly* was among those who reacted negatively to the book's depiction of adultery—including its physical aspects—writing, "With nice economy the book is called *Couples.* It would have been more precise to have called it *Coupling*" (129). Updike in a later interview somewhat bemusedly characterized Trilling's response as "a banshee cry of indignation" and contrasted it with the "soothing, complimentary" reactions of his fellow citizens (*Conversations* 25) of Ipswich, Massachusetts, on which Tarbox was based.

Couples is among the more sophisticated of his works in its narrative, with a first-person limited narration that moves easily among the minds of several of its many characters (there are ten couples) yet focuses most on Piet Hannema, a more vital version of Rabbit Angstrom who works as a contractor more interested in the renovation of old homes than in the more profitable building of new, tacky houses. An early section moves into the consciousness of Foxy Whitman, one of Updike's most convincing female characters, then shifts to Piet making love to Georgene Thorne, also a convincing character.

In the course of the novel Piet becomes a casual adulterer, presented as not that different from many of his acquaintances, at least in his sexual aspirations.

His main act of unfaithfulness, however, is not so much in the several women he beds as in his taking on the winterization and strengthening of a cottage overlooking a salt marsh that he had declined to rebuild for his beautiful but distant wife, Angela. Descended from whaling captains, Angela had longed for a home with an ocean view; Piet, orphan of Dutch Reformed greenhouse owners from western Michigan who were killed in a traffic accident about ten years before the time of the novel, has been content with a more limited, traditional place, an eighteenth-century farmhouse with a barn and outdoor basketball court on two acres. Piet is an immigrant to Massachusetts via his army friendship with Matt Gallagher, who becomes his somewhat uneasy partner in realty and building. "All houses, all things that enclosed, pleased Piet, but his modest Dutch sense of how much of the world he was permitted to mark off and hold was precisely satisfied by this lot two hundred feet back from the road, a mile from the center of town, four miles distant from the sea" (5). This sense of grace within limitation tends to make Piet a sympathetic character despite his departures from the straight and narrow.

The former summer cottage that Piet now renovates is owned by the Whitmans, younger new arrivals in town. They buy it via Matt Gallagher for its view of the salt marshes and in spite of what Piet identifies as "a wind exposure that would defy all insulation" (5). Having already been jacked up to add a new first story, the house is a money pit. Everything in it requires reconstruction at huge expense, from crumbling cellar to heating system to kitchen to roof, which is why Piet had declined to rebuild it for Angela. His eventual affair with Foxy Whitman proceeds in parallel with her first pregnancy and the rebuilding of the house. This and other plot points of the novel are counterpointed by such ominous outside events as the sinking of the U.S. nuclear submarine *Thresher*, on April 9, 1963 (31), labor unrest in the steel industry (76), and the assassination of President Kennedy on November 22, 1963 (294), the day of one of the couples' planned parties, which is not canceled since the liquor already had been bought. The Great Alaska Earthquake of March 27, 1964, is also mentioned as Piet and Angela discuss their divorce (404).

An earlier slump in the stock market of April–May 1962 is identified with the beginning of mate swapping between "the Applesmiths" (109), the Applebys and the Smiths, nicknamed "little-Smiths" to differentiate them from another Smith couple who had been members of an earlier Tarbox coterie. This is the prototype for several subsequent pairings. The reader already intuits that the couples of the title will in their turn be succeeded by new, younger, hipper people to come—as indeed proves to be the case at the novel's end.

Updike's characteristic concern with mortality is well handled, particularly so on a small scale, as in the death of the Hannema children's hamster (76). This death is more affecting than the off-stage death from cancer late in the novel of brilliant North Korean defector physicist John Ong, half of one of the more peripheral of the ten couples. Ong's death makes no difference to those at the center of the novel, while the hamster's death touches Piet's younger daughter, Nancy, aged five, and so also touches Piet, to the extent that he can be touched. Nancy let the animal out of its cage to play in a makeshift pen, and the family cat kills it, though Nancy knows that she is responsible. The death prompts Piet to build a new, more secure enclosure of novel, modernist design for the next hamster. Angela does not even recognize it as a cage, which helps to suggest their essential incompatibility of perception. The pairing of Ong's death with that of the hamster also suggests that there is something more important to Piet in emotions—particularly his own—than in the world of scientific rationalism represented by Ong or by Foxy's husband, a seemingly perfect PhD biologist trying to find a topic on the cutting edge of research and consistently failing to do so.

Piet is uncomfortable in the worlds of profit and loss represented by Frank Appleby (a trust officer) and Harold Smith (a broker) or by his partner Matt and their rising young foreman, Leon Jazinski. While spotting Jazinski's talent for organization early on and insisting to Gallagher that they keep him on at all costs, Piet really is more in tune with his elderly employees Adams and Comeau, Mutt and Jeff–like old carpenters who can spend weeks on making a new garage perfect, even to the point of painstakingly reworking already adequate factory-made windows. The two carpenters live in their own world of traditional craftsmanship, one with which Piet sympathizes; in sympathy with Piet they have nicknamed his partner "Greedy Gally" (87). Much as he is uncomfortable with Matt's concern with profit, Piet also is uncomfortable around the black backhoe operator who rips out an Indian burial ground in the process of digging foundations for three new houses. Essentially the only reference to the civil rights concerns of these years is Piet's "Pardon me, Dr. King" (86), in association with his stereotyping of this minor character. Tarbox's residents are almost all white, with only the Ongs breaking the color line.

Religion is ironically inscribed on the street plan of Tarbox, with the Congregational Church sited on Divinity Street and many businesses on Charity, its cross street (80). Other streets include Prudence and Temperance (443), also ironic names given novel's subject. Of the ten couples, only Piet and Foxy seem to be churchgoers, while Angela is an active skeptic regarding religion. The beginning of Piet and Foxy's affair is surrounded by religion, though perhaps not entirely auspiciously: he sees her leaving the Episcopal Church, burning rubber in her husband's black MG sports car, on Palm Sunday. She decides to call to ask him to remodel her house a week later, on Easter Sunday.

Interestingly Updike found religion to be an inspiration for the novel on many levels, and he was quite pragmatic about its serving the book's composition in his *Paris Review* interview: "I guess I'm never unconscious of myself as a writer and of my present project. A few places are specially conducive to inspiration—automobiles, church—private places. I plotted *Couples* almost entirely in church—little shivers and urgencies I would note down on the program and carry down to the office Monday" (*Conversations* 30).

The most notable set-piece of the novel is the burning of the Congregational church in the rain. After the church is struck by lightning, fire smolders inside and then breaks out in an appropriate parallel to the sexual intrigues of the novel; only the pediment, cupola, and rooster weathercock survive. The burning becomes a public spectacle with everyone in town turning out to watch, but there is no religious feeling in the event. The poisonously acerbic dentist and procurator of then still-illegal abortions, Freddy Thorne, brings a beer to drink while he watches, and Piet casually ends up sleeping with Carol Constantine afterward, perceiving her body much as he perceived that of Freddy's wife, Georgene, his first mistress, early on in the novel. Characteristically he seems more affected by the old, lost craftsmanship of the ruined church than by the lost values that its destruction may represent. Almost at the end of the novel, the antique weathercock is rescued from atop its ruined steeple by a daring young construction worker hanging from the ball of a crane. Early in the novel, the weathercock's penny eye is identified with the eye of God (17), but late in the book the eye of God seems not to be watching: "The sky above was empty but for two parallel jet trails" (457).

Piet leaves Tarbox (with Foxy, his new wife) and apparently finds happiness in Lexington, where he moves to take a federal job as a construction inspector arranged by Foxy's father. In one of the Maples stories, "Gesturing" (1974), Updike gives Piet a brief appearance, unnamed but recognizable as "the ginger-haired contractor" who had built a "mock-antique wing" to a local restaurant some twelve years before "and then left town, bankrupt but oddly cheerful. His memory hovered between the beams" (*Early Stories* 807). This is another suggestion of the unity of Updike's fictional world: a character may recur in separate works without breaking the spell, even as characters may move across wide expanses of time.

The critical conversation regarding the novel has noted its religious elements particularly, seeing Piet as a soul (Hannema/anima) caught between the significantly named Angela, whom he neither derives sexual satisfaction from nor feels closeness to, and the more vital Foxy, with whom he eventually finds happiness of a secular and carnal variety. Piet is the only of his friends who goes to church, and he worries about becoming one of the "builders burying the world God made" (83). Updike made clear the novel's religious theme in his gloss of the denouement:

> A god who is not God the Creator is not very real to me, so that, yes, it cer-
> tainly is God who throws the lightning bolt, and this God is above the nice
> god, above the god we can worship and empathize with. I guess I'm saying
> there's a fierce God above the kind God, and he's the one Piet believes in.
> At any rate, when the church is burned, Piet is relieved of morality and can
> choose Foxy—or can accept the choice made for him by Foxy and Angela
> operating in unison—can move out of the paralysis of guilt into what after
> all is a kind of freedom. He divorces the supernatural to marry the natural.
> I wanted the loss of Angela to be felt as a real loss—Angela is nicer than
> Foxy—nevertheless it is Foxy that he most deeply wants, it is Foxy who in
> some obscure way was turned on the lathe for him. So that the book does
> have a happy ending. (Conversations 33)

CHAPTER 5

The Shadow of Nathaniel Hawthorne and New England Puritanism
The Eastwick and Scarlet Letter Novels

Religion continues as a concern in Updike's novels derived from New England Puritanism and Nathaniel Hawthorne's *The Scarlet Letter*. A long-time mainline Protestant, Updike traces both secular and religious responses to mortality. In the highly satirical *Witches of Eastwick* (1984), the devilish Darryl Van Horne is a bumbling connoisseur of art, collecting indiscriminately an exquisite Alberto Giacometti and robust Auguste Rodin as well as technically suspect pop-art icons such as Ed Keinholz and Niki de Saint Phalle. (Perhaps not surprising, Van Horne prefers the trendy and specious, for example highly praising Keinholz's sculpture depicting sex in the back seat of a 1938 Dodge.) Art decidedly seems not to be the answer to life's questions in this novel, but neither does religion. The pastor in the novel becomes a radical left-wing bomber, leaving his theologically untrained wife to take over his congregation—and she in turn is tormented by the three witches, the protagonists of the novel.

Like *Couples*, *The Witches of Eastwick* explores how Updike's characters deal with the breakdown of conventional moral standards, including those governing sexuality. Unlike that earlier novel, though, *Witches* marks a movement in Updike's work away from a more strictly male point of view as the author worked to portray women in this new world. Reviewers had previously criticized his female characters, and they split on this effort in *Witches*: some found the novel misogynistic, while others felt it to be a highly successful satirical send-up of patriarchy. (Updike returned to his three witches and themes of mortality in his final published novel, *The Widows of Eastwick*.)

The Eastwick witches are identified by Updike as partial descendants of Anne Hutchinson, the woman who challenged the teachings of the Puritan divines in 1600s Massachusetts Bay Colony. Hutchinson was a prototype for Hawthorne's strongest female character, Hester Prynne, in *The Scarlet Letter* (1850), and Updike mines some of the same veins of religion and guilt as the earlier author. Updike explored the implications for twentieth-century American life of Hawthorne's ideas and characters. As with the Rabbit novels, he wrote a series of novels inspired by Hawthorne, a trilogy with each book inspired by one of the main characters of *The Scarlet Letter*, Hester, Arthur Dimmesdale, and Roger Chillingworth.

A Month of Sundays

A Month of Sundays was Updike's first attempt to deal directly with Hawthorne's influence on American and New England thought. As often was the case for Updike, it was an experiment of sorts, in this case using the form of the diary of Rev. Tom Marshfield, a young clergyman sent on retreat in an attempt to cure his somewhat aimless philandering among the women of his flock. Updike used the diary format in order to give a sense of spontaneity and life to his narration but also in hopes of producing the novel quickly after having expended an inordinate amount of time on the unsuccessful *Buchanan Dying* (*Conversations,* 131). Tom's diary is a prescribed element in his retreat, intended to be penitential but perhaps not succeeding, as he finds himself giving in to sometimes salacious puns. In addition to Tom's diary, the novel also includes sermons (as does *The Witches of Eastwick*), and in general it is something of a romp, despite its tips of the hat to Christian theology and the New England tradition. Reviewing it for *The New York Times,* Anatole Broyard characterized the book as suffering "from the author's own mixed feelings. He wants to have his communion wafer and eat it, too: one senses that he would like to take some of these issues to heart, but his sophistication won't let him. The result is an ambivalent comedy, one that the author resolves with a really atrocious punch line."

Updike characterized the novel as a retelling of *The Scarlet Letter,* even including some direct quotations from Hawthorne's novel salted into his own narrative. He explained Hawthorne's importance and appeal in a 1980 interview with Charlie Reilly: "I think that even though there may be greater American books—let's say, for the sake of argument, *Moby-Dick* and *Huckleberry Finn*—*The Scarlet Letter* somehow sticks in my mind as the first American masterpiece. Among other things, it masterfully considers the problems of religion, the plight of woman in general, the problems of a fascinating woman in particular. It's amazingly well written, too. The more I read it, the more I'm struck by how 'right' everything is" (*Conversations* 129).

Updike has set a daunting challenge for himself, and in his attempt to go head to head with one of America's great romancers, he seems to blink. Humor becomes his escape from the challenge, enabling him to avoid high seriousness in dealing with the themes that Hawthorne weaves into his narrative. In *The Witches of Eastwick,* Updike more successfully fuses comedy and seriousness in pursuit of these concerns.

Roger's Version

The second of Updike's novels directly inspired by *The Scarlet Letter, Roger's Version,* is narrated by fifty-three-year-old Roger Lambert. He is a professor of divinity in an unnamed eastern city and somewhat echoes Hawthorne's Roger Chillingworth in his often cold and overly calculating approach to life. Lambert had fallen from the active clergy into a faculty position via an extramarital affair with the petite and perfect Esther, precisely one hundred pounds, who has been his wife for fourteen years in the present time of the novel, which is set just after the reelection of President Ronald Reagan in 1984. They have a son in middle school, Ritchie, who apparently is learning disabled—or at least a victim of math anxiety—and a source of some worry to both of them.

Into Roger's office and life comes Dale Koehler, a young computer science major convinced that he can prove the existence of God via computer analysis of the mathematical constants underlying the principles of physics. As Lambert echoes the aging Chillingworth, Dale somewhat echoes *The Scarlet Letter*'s passionate young clergyman, Arthur Dimmesdale. Roger is uninterested in Dale's proposal, seeing his quest as a form of heresy, but passes him along to the divinity school's fellowship-granting committee as a means of getting rid of him. Of course this is not the effect; Dale becomes increasingly involved in Roger's household and eventually is granted his fellowship to prove scientifically the existence of God.

Dale also is a friend of nineteen-year-old Verna Ekelof, daughter of Roger's half-sister and mother of an illegitimate, half-black baby, Paula. Verna has moved to the city in order to escape the family home in Cleveland, which is located in a public housing project. While the somewhat cold Roger previously has managed to avoid Verna since her arrival, her connection with Dale brings her into his household for Thanksgiving dinner. Dale becomes both math tutor to Ritchie and lover to Esther (if the reader is to believe that Roger's very detailed narration of the affair is not a figment of his aging imagination), while Verna becomes a project of both Roger and Esther. He encourages her in her pursuit of a GED and art lessons, and she arranges for baby Paula to be admitted to the day care center where she works so that Verna will have more time for her studies. Roger also finds himself sexually attracted to Verna, and Verna is not above using that attraction to manipulate Roger to her own advantage.

Plot complications include Dale's loss of faith in his computer project (and perhaps in God) and Verna's abuse of her baby, which leads to a greenstick fracture, a trip to the emergency room in Roger's Volvo, the attention of child protective services, and, eventually, Paula's incorporation into the Lambert household. In a graceful coda to the novel's action, Roger takes the now somewhat more sophisticated Verna to lunch at a sixtieth-story restaurant overlooking the elegiacally described city, an unnamed but recognizable Boston. Roger also buys Verna an airline ticket back to Cleveland, where she and Dale may perhaps take up life together in the heartland in a prefiguration of Pru and Nelson's move to Akron in *Rabbit Remembered.* The ending is convincing in its evocation of Verna's increased (but not complete) maturity, of Roger's coming to peace with his aging and the aftermath of his sleeping with Verna, of Ritchie's greater contentedness in becoming like an older brother to Paula, and of the sense that an orderly, more mature existence has come to both Roger and Esther.

The Witches of Eastwick

The Witches of Eastwick is among Updike's most audacious and successful novels, one likely to continue to engage reader interest in the future. He wrote it partly in response to some reviewers' objections that his novels focus primarily on male protagonists and thus make female characters subsidiary and not well developed, the most famous example of this being Diana Trilling's negative review of *Couples.* Like novels such as the later *Brazil,* it also represents an exploration of the magical realist genre originally associated with South American writers such as Gabriel García Márquez, in which realistic and fantastic elements coexist and are presented as possessing equal credibility and validity. It is engaging in its characterization, challenging in its ideas, and enthralling in its craftsmanship.

The novel has four main characters: the three titular witches and a mysterious personage who comes to their seaside Connecticut town. Eastwick is modeled probably on Ipswich, Massachusetts, where Updike lived for many years. All the witches are in their thirties, divorced, and have multiple children, who are mostly not considered in the novel in any important way. They are more encumbrances to the main characters rather than characters in their own right, "so awkward and needy, plucking, clinging, looking . . . for nurture" (71). The coven that the three women form (meeting Thursday evenings for food, fellowship, and a little witchery, including the raising of their ambiguously described "cone of power") is the important element in their lives, giving them a way to deal with the difficulties of being unattached women in a society that still expects people to come as if creatures just off the biblical Ark, two by two. Their husbands are rather ambiguously out of the picture. While the novel intimates early on that the witches have been divorced, it also suggests that the husbands were rendered unimportant and possibly transmuted into inanimate domestic objects, two into herblike powders suitable for seasoning the odd menu item and one into a placemat, and a plasticized one at that. The novel at first seems teasingly to hint that the witchcraft is just a metaphor, but as the story develops, it comes to seem more and more the real thing, with telling influence over the physical world and even the power to bring death.

Of the three women, Alexandra (Lexa) Spofford, the oldest at thirty-eight and the mother of four, is the novel's rather sympathetic protagonist. Lexa is most in tune with the forces of nature, and early on in a wonderful set-piece covering roughly four pages, she conjures a thunderstorm to clear the public beach of annoying and mostly teenaged interlopers who are preventing her from taking her Labrador retriever for a walk off-leash. Conjuring the storm begins with an evocation of what nature and her power over it mean to Alexandra:

> Not until midlife did she truly believe that she had a right to exist, that the forces of nature had created her not as an afterthought and companion—a bent rib . . . —but as the mainstay of the continuing Creation. . . . Alexandra closed her eyes while Coal shivered and whimpered in fright and she willed this vast interior of herself . . . to generate an interface of lightning between tall walls of air. And the sky in the north did rumble, so faintly only Coal could hear. (14–15)

> Invisibly Alexandra grew huge, in a kind of maternal wrath gathering all the sheaves of this becalmed September world to herself, and the lids of her eyes flew open as if at a command. A blast of cold air hit from the north, the approach of a front that whipped the desultory pennants of the distant boathouse straight out from their staffs. (15)

> Her face from hairline to chin streamed and all the colors of the rainbow were in this liquid film, because of the agitation of her aura. Lightning kept taking her photograph. (16–17)

> To the eyes of the young people huddled with their sodden gritty towels and ignominious goosebumps . . . Alexandra appeared miraculously dry, not a hair of her massive braid out of place, not a patch of her brocaded jacket

damp. It was just such unverifiable impressions that spread among us in Eastwick the rumor of witchcraft. (18)

Updike is at the top of his form in narrative style in this novel, another of the many factors leading to its artistic and commercial success. *The Witches of Eastwick* continually surprises. To take another humorous example, all three witches have familiar companions, but they all are dogs rather than more traditionally expected cats, one of a number of small changes in what readers expect from witchcraft tales that Updike introduces to his material.

Alexandra comes to value herself despite continuing doubts, and she unleashes power. She is large, impressive, and thoughtful, fallen into East Coast adulthood—via attendance at New London's Connecticut College for Women—from a childhood in the western United States in which she was the most treasured child of her father, a Levi's salesman. Apparently no man since has measured up, although Alexandra has not given up looking. Her mother had faded away and died early in Alexandra's life, offering her no clear female role model to follow. The novel seems to intimate that this was to the good, producing a strong personality not so limited by conventional female roles. In her appearance and in her search for a place as a woman in a male-dominated society, Lexa resembles nineteenth-century feminist author Margaret Fuller (1810–1850), who was much admired by Hawthorne and was the basis for the exotic and beautiful Zenobia of the usually underrated *The Blithedale Romance* (1852) and one of the inspirations for Hester Prynne. Lexa also resembles another source figure for Hester, Anne Hutchinson, who is mentioned in the first chapter of Updike's novel and who was expelled by the Massachusetts Bay Colony's Puritan patriarchs for preaching her own Antinomian version of Christianity to women in weekly meetings in her home that somewhat prefigure the weekly coven meetings of Updike's characters. Like Lexa, Hutchinson earlier came to Roger Williams's Connecticut, which was a haven for the unorthodox, and settled in waterfront Portsmouth, somewhat echoed in fictional Eastwick, also situated on the water.

Like all three of Updike's witches, Lexa is an creator of sorts, a college fine arts major and self-taught sculptor of compact female figures of fired clay that recall both naked Paleolithic fertility symbols and the brightly painted larger works of Niki de Saint Phalle. An extended motif of the novel derives from avant-garde pop art of the decade, making excellent use of Updike's interest in art and his time as a reviewer. Lexa's "bubbies" are of great power, "chunky female bodies four or five inches long, often faceless and without feet, coiled or bent in recumbent positions and heavier than expected when held in the hand" (19). They comfort their buyers and sell reasonably well at Eastwick's two boutique galleries appealing largely to vacationers, the Yapping Fox and the Hungry Sheep.

Brunette Jane Smart (nicknamed "Jane Pain" by the other two for her tart personality and generally negative outlook on the world) is the second oldest, at age thirty-two. She is a cellist, probably the most serious artist of the three. Her art uplifts but also tortures her through the endless practice that further warps her already distressingly asymmetrical body structure. She is the most stereotypically witchy of the three, with a characteristic sinister, sibilant hiss as she speaks. At times in interior monologues she expresses her antipathy for the greats of classical music such as Johann Sebastian Bach, "this dead square-faced old Lutheran with his wig and his Lord and his genius and two wives and seventeen children, not caring how the tips of her fingers hurt or how her obedient spirit was pushed back and forth, up and down, by these military notes just to give him a voice after death, a bully's immortality" (76). The patriarchy is not her friend, and a continuing strand in the novel suggests that women fall from girlhood into marriage, "destined to become beauties and slaves" (116) in the voice of Updike's narrator, who seems to represent the common opinion of Eastwick's townspeople, perhaps in an echo of the narration of William Faulkner's eerie short story "A Rose for Emily" (1930), another tale of thwarted and distorted female aspiration. Jane's characterization of Bach is just one example of this slavery.

Unlike Lexa's solitary sculpting, Jane's musical performance requires intimate interaction with other human beings, not just boutique sales outlets. In Eastwick concert-grade classical musicians are rare on the ground and not well compensated. Jane thus makes ends meet by giving music lessons; she also associates herself with the Unitarian and other churches as choir director; with Raymond Neff, high school music teacher and leader of the local string ensemble; and with Greta, Neff's unappealingly Germanic wife, possibly a member of a competing coven. That both women are sleeping with Raymond adds another conflict.

Redheaded Sukie (Susannah) Rougemont is the youngest (though also thirty-two, like Jane); the most conventionally attractive, charming, and youthful in appearance; and the most social of the three witches. Indeed her job as reporter for the *Eastwick Word* requires interaction with others, which Sukie loves rather than merely endures. She is hardly an artist with the written word (or an apostle of the religious word). One of the most telling and subtle characterizations in the novel is achieved via Updike's inclusion of a feature article she writes, with all of her misspellings of the names of actual artists, misplaced modifiers, and generally breathless and less than objective tone. She is forgiving and nurturing, and she thinks of men as "this other race interwoven with hers, so full of bravado and dirty tough talk but such babies really" (137).

The subject of Sukie's feature article is Darryl Van Horne, forty-two years old, newly arrived in town from New York City and a would-be inventor of solar power devices. Once a child prodigy pianist, he partners with Jane in musical duets and sexual ones—not to mention more expansive couplings. He also is a lover and collector of some of the tawdriest of 1960s pop art: "gaudy travesties of the ordinary—giant pay telephones in limp canvas, American flags duplicated in impasto, oversize dollar bills rendered with deadpan fidelity, plaster eyeglasses with not eyes but parted lips behind the lenses, relentless enlargements of our comic strips and advertising insignia, our movie stars and our bottle caps, our candies and newspapers and traffic signs. . . . permanized garbage" (87). Keinholz's *Back Seat Dodge '38* gets a detailed and appreciative exposition from Darryl, though he seems to miss the satirical social criticism embodied in Keinholz's artwork and does not own the work in question. Darryl praises only the details and ignores Keinholz's criticism of the ways in which the young were then forced to experience sex. He consistently misses the point with this and other serious works of art that appear in the novel. Indeed his abiding interest in art is as a surefire investment.

Darryl is, it comes to seem, the devil. Very early in the novel, it is established that Lexa is destined for him, or rather he for her. "As in a crystal ball she saw that she would meet and fall in love with this man, and nothing good would come of it" (4). In one of the novel's neatest touches, everything about Darryl is somewhat tacky and misshapen, beginning with his hairy hands that look more like rubber gloves than human appendages and continuing through his entire scruffy and oily-haired person. His understanding of the physics of solar power is at best rudimentary (he hopes to find a loophole in the second law of thermodynamics, entropy), and in fact his electrical experiments never succeed—or measure up to Lexa's control of nature as she creates the thunderstorm. Everything about him falls apart. His assistant, Fidel Malaguer, somewhat echoes the Igor henchman character of classic horror movies as well as Aminadab, the more sensible servant to misguided scientist Aylmer in Hawthorne's "The Birth-Mark" (1843), the tale of a man who tries to make perfect the woman he loves but ends by killing her in a reversal of the tale of Pygmalion. Most commentators view Hawthorne's story at least partly as a criticism of hopes for scientific progress and human perfectibility. In another echo of Hawthorne's tale, the most nearly perfect character in Updike's novel will later die after marrying Darryl.

Taking over a decaying local mansion—probably based on Ipswich's Castle Hill estate and perhaps also on the Beverley Farms, Massachusetts, mansion Updike lived in with his second wife, Martha—Darryl rehabs it as combination residence and laboratory. He installs a giant hot tub into a remodeled conservatory now equipped with a retractable roof and a supposedly waterproof stereo system that progressively declines in function as the story proceeds. The hot tub is intended to be shared with the witches, but orgies typically are interrupted by Darryl's bare-bottomed attempts to repair the stereo as it shorts out from the humidity, and the witches find more pleasure in each other than in him.

Darryl also hires contractors to erect a dome-covered tennis court, filling a marshy inlet to create the space for it, notwithstanding the presence of nesting, legally protected snowy egrets. Very much unlike Lexa, he cares nothing for nature. On the court Darryl and the witches play a doubles game that becomes half tennis match, half witchcraft one-upmanship—one of the few scenes in the novel adapted faithfully in the 1987 film version of *Witches* starring Cher, Susan Sarandon, Michelle Pfeiffer, and Jack Nicholson. As the novel develops, the tennis court's air-supported dome gradually deflates and is abandoned, part of a pattern of decrepitude and decay associated with the devil. Darryl's impressive off-white Mercedes has a fender repainted in a shade just far enough from matching to depress its value, with another fender still dented. Many of his artwork possessions are "from the school of" rather than the real thing, and his Mies van der Rohe glass-topped table is chipped. As a pianist, despite his skill he tends toward "Tiptoe through the Tulips" and odd-tempo versions of classics: "The a Nightingale Sang in Berkeley Square Boogie," "The High How the Moon March," and the Beatles' "Yesterday" in the rhythms of a samba (123–34). Beauty disturbs him, and he takes refuge in shallow parody. Later in the book he delivers a guest sermon to the Unitarians, largely on the horror of bodily parasites, titled "This Is a Horrible Creation."

In one of a number of comic touches, Updike describes Lexa's black lab, Coal, as always attempting to understand what is going on around him but never quite succeeding and then intimates that Darryl himself is similarly doglike and uncomprehending of the world. It seems that just as in the affairs of ordinary human beings, the devil really has only as much power as the witches grant him and none of his own save the powers to flatter and mislead.

Updike's exploration of witchcraft walks a line between two views of the practice: as sinister worship of the devil and as a more comprehensible and sympathetic remnant of earlier forms of nature worship. The tension between these two perspectives adds interest to the novel and also makes it more accessible to readers. While witchcraft in the novel is not pure Satanism, it has the sting of evil and its real consequences. The witches themselves seem divided in their views of witchcraft, with Lexa clearly an earth-mother type whose power is related to her sympathy with and understanding of the forces of nature. Jane seems more malevolent and devil-worshipping. She casts the spell that apparently kills Jenny Gabriel, the physically perfect younger woman who comes to compete with the witches for Darryl's attention and marries him. Sukie is naive and charming, rather a fellow traveler in the magical arts than a mistress of them, with particular power to enchant somewhat clueless men, though all three women have affairs. As the narrator wittily notes, "Being a divorcee in a small town is a little like playing Monopoly; eventually you land on all the properties" (25).

Each witch can cause death, as when Lexa sacrifices scuttling crabs on the beach as a part of the spell when she conjures the storm. She also kills an annoying, barking puppy, which she immediately regrets when she realizes it was only lonely and that she could easily have used her powers to free it from its tether. One of Sukie's affairs leads to two unintentional deaths. Her more characteristic spell is a love fetish intended to join Lexa and Darryl. Only Jane malevolently sets out to kill.

That Updike was a lifelong observant Christian and interested in questions of faith and disbelief perhaps helps to explain his sometimes satirical exploration of both versions of witchcraft. He seems equally willing to be skeptical about modern versions of Christianity. This is seen notably in the person of the wonderfully named Rev. Ed Parsley, the woefully ineffectual Unitarian pastor who wishes to join the counterculture despite being over thirty and thus not really eligible. Reverend Parsley abandons church and family to run off to join "the Movement" with a rather hapless young local woman and ends by blowing himself up in an urban bomb factory. (Parsley is identified by the fingerprints of the only remnant of him left after the explosion, a hand.) His wife, Brenda, succeeds him as pastor of the church, more because no one can find a graceful way to evict her from the parsonage than for her theological training. She has none, but she looks the part of a religious leader once out of the miniskirts that Ed had insisted she wear as a part of his misguided search for youth, and her sermons are no worse than his.

The first of the three sections of the novel is a charming tour de force of description and satire; situations turn more serious in the second part of the novel. Sukie's affair with her alcoholic, middle-aged newspaper editor boss, Clyde Gabriel, leads to his suicide and murder of his once-perky and appealing wife, Felicia, who had become an earnestly upright, misanthropic, and hectoring busybody, whom Jane and Sukie have tormented by throwing trash into a cookie jar that has become a magical portal into Felicia's mouth. (Pastor Brenda Parsley suffers the same torment at times.)

To Clyde, who searches in vain for God and nightly reads Roman poet and philosopher Lucretius in the original Latin, Sukie is heaven and Felicia hell. In Lucretius's *De Rerum Natura* (The Nature of Things), Clyde learns that death is nothing, since even the mind is mortal, and he kills his hectoring wife on what should be the resistible impulse of a moment. Updike's description of the murder echoes and perhaps parodies Lucretius's discussion of the possibility of free will. Felicia has been spitting out odd little feathers, thumbtacks, and the like, as unaccounted for and unappealing as her self-righteous opinions, and the Gabriels' marriage has become "like two people locked up with one lesson to read, over and over, until the words become madness" (149). There seem to be no happy marriages in the novel.

The deaths of the Gabriels bring to town their young adult children, Jenny and Chris, respectively a Chicago x-ray technician and a not very successful gay New York actor, to settle the estate and sell their parents' house. They are also pulled into the orbit of the coven and Darryl. At first Jenny seems to be Lexa's rival, and indeed she eventually marries Darryl, shutting out Lexa, though in the end Chris proves a more apt sexual partner for him. The witches cast a spell on Jenny in revenge for the marriage, the malignancy prosaically sealed into a waxen fetish figure with Reynolds Wrap, and Jenny declines into death from metastatic cancer, which had been Lexa's great fear for herself. It is in character that Jane is the leader in this revenge while Lexa eventually attempts to reverse the spell, but this proves no more possible than bringing back the barking puppy or a squirrel she had struck down in a similar moment of pique.

Neatly organized, the novel covers a year, 1968–69, following the cycle of life from autumn to autumn, with the first of its three sections appropriately ending late on Halloween night and the final major plot point being the death of Jenny Gabriel the next year, just after Labor Day. In the end Darryl disappears back to New York City with Chris as his lover, earlier rumors of his homosexuality having apparently proven true, and leaves a heap of unpaid bills for renovations. One major creditor is Lexa's happily married yet straying plumber-lover, Joe Marino, who had crafted the entire hot tub and surroundings on credit. The witches realize that Darryl has played them and that Eastwick is a trap for them. In the end they all leave town, each having found or conjured an appropriate new husband and a more or less happy marriage. Lexa's new husband is a lean westerner, a potter from Taos conjured out of dried western mud she scrapes from under a pickup truck's fender. Bostonian Jane's is a scion of a rich old Brookline family (and son of a witch, as Updike reveals in the novel's sequel). Upstate New Yorker Sukie's new husband is a salesman of a then-new invention, the computer word processor, on one of which she begins a new and successful career as a romance novelist in which her stylistic infelicities count for nothing.

The Widows of Eastwick

Updike returns to the three women again, thirty-some years later, in one of his last novels, the worthy but not quite so transcendently wonderful *The Widows of Eastwick* (2008). Having drifted apart after their marriages, they reconnect as widows, their Christmas notes and occasional phone calls leading again to closer contact as their husbands pass away, one after another. The first to be widowed is Lexa, and one of her first steps "as a wife suddenly liberated into solitude, was to travel—as if the world at large, by way of flimsy boarding cards and tedious airport delays, and the faint but undeniable risk of flight . . . could be compelled to yield the fruitful aggravation of having a mate" (3). She takes a ten-day train and bus tour of the Canadian Rockies and finds herself in a group made up mostly of Australian couples, who have no place for a single woman and who trust what they read in their guidebooks more than what Lexa tells them from firsthand knowledge of New England, a coming stage of their North American tour. There also is a Malay couple who get lost with Lexa while hiking near Lake Jasper and whose main character trait seems to be their accent, which leads them to replace the *l* sound with an *r*. (e.g., on a glacier excursion: "The grare is terrible" [21]), an unfortunately stereotypical piece of comic business that Updike also utilized in *Rabbit at Rest*. Lexa finds the Malays as uninteresting as the Aussies find her, and so she pays little attention to them as people rather than stereotypes. In another display of Lexa's limitations, her interest is piqued by the one single man on the tour, a doppelgänger of her lean, dead husband, but as soon as she learns that Tennessean Willard McHugh is gay, still grieving the loss of his partner of forty-seven years, she dismisses them as "a pair of fairies" (25) and flatly turns down Willard's evening offer of a drink, conversation, and possible sexual activity. Stereotype again wins out, uncharacteristically for the perceptive Lexa, who usually can read people's auras as well as their characters—unless her emotions are involved, as with her decades-earlier liaison with Darryl Van Horne.

The "tour mother" for the Canadian excursion is the condescending, frizzy-haired and ironically named (for a mountain tour guide) Heidi. The high point of the tour for Lexa at first seems to be her own discovery of the loonie and toonie, Canada's practical one and two dollar coins. There is a literal and more important high point after the tour group's gondola ride to the top of Sulphur Mountain in Banff National Park, when Lexa, alone for a few moments, walks the boardwalk to Sanson's Peak and feels that she is flying above everything. "She was above and among endless gentle mountains; they were her friends, a grand Other holding her in Its hand. Nature was within her and around her and infinite" (28–29). As in *The Witches of Eastwick,* nature and Lexa are made for each other and closely identified.

There are overtones in this description of New England transcendentalist Ralph Waldo Emerson (1803–82) and his famous essay of contemplative philosophy "Nature" (1836), in which a philosopher sits on a hilltop and so closely identifies with nature that only the thin membrane of his eyeball separates him from it: "Standing on the bare ground,—my head bathed by the blithe air, and uplifted into infinite space,—all mean egotism vanishes. I become a transparent eye-ball; I am nothing; I see all; the currents of the Universal Being circulate through me; I am part and particle of God"(8). Lexa later characterizes her mountaintop moment as a religious experience. Overall, though, solo traveling is not Lexa's thing.

The next to be widowed is Jane, and as companions Jane and Lexa launch into a more adventurous journey to the prototypic land of the dead, Egypt (at Jane's suggestion, and despite Lexa's fear of possible post-9/11 terrorist attack). Their Nile excursion, as members of another group tour, takes them to the expected places, including the Valley of the Kings. (Earlier Lexa takes an ill-advised and comical circumnavigation of the Great Pyramid on camelback.) They explore tombs, and from the deck of their tour boat at day's end, Jane fells a bat out of a flitting flock with an impromptu spell. In the land of the pharaohs, mortality is all about. They find the Nile cruise quite relaxing, and Jane proposes that all three witches get together for further travel.

A couple of months later Sukie also is a widow, with the intimation that malevolent Jane has quietly cast a death spell on her husband to free her for adventure, and the three witches tour China, where everything is "more or less astonishing, beginning with their being here at all, on the other side of the world" (80). They walk the Great Wall in conical straw hats purchased by still-whimsical Sukie, tour Peking, including Mao's tomb and the Forbidden City, view the Emperor Ch'in's vast funerary army of ceramic soldiers, and feel liberated from the constraints of Christianity: "Here, the air felt clear of that particular history, of those tyrannical ghosts preaching sin and salvation, and the Godforsaken women in their impudent tourism felt free" (100). As in the earlier tour of Egypt, intimations of mortality are all about, and now their coven is reconstituted. They thus return to Eastwick, renting for the summer two apartments in Darryl's former mansion, now divided up into condos.

This journey to their past is also a journey into family relationships for Lexa. Her lumpish older daughter, Marcy, still lives in Eastwick. A late-in-life mother now over fifty, Marcy has settled into a prosaic middle-class marriage to an electrician with an ambition to retire to Florida and own a boat of some sort (echoing Lexa's own tradesman lover, plumber Joe Marino, from the earlier novel). When Marcy telephones to inquire about the witches' plans, Lexa professes the desire not to intrude on her by spending the summer in town as Jane had suggested; Marcy vehemently proclaims her desire for a closer connection to Lexa for herself and her two sons "while spilling out . . . absurd resentment, as if her mother were God and had created the universe" (119). In a telling passage, Lexa explains to her daughter the rationale for witchcraft, and perhaps Updike's own rationale for treating it in the earlier novel: "Girls your age just can't realize how few opportunities there were for women when I was young. Our job was to make babies and buy American consumer goods. If we fell off the marriage bandwagon, there was nothing much left for us but to ride a broomstick and cook up spells. Don't look so shocked, it was *power*. Everybody needs power. Otherwise the world eats you up" (160–61). Sukie earlier had made a similar point to Lexa, suggesting that it would be safe to return to Eastwick: "Hexes don't last forever. That poisonous atmosphere had to do with the times, the Sixties decaying into the Seventies, and with us being young and still full of juice and stuck in the middle class" (113).

Once persuaded and back in Eastwick and given the nicest bedroom in their condo (with an appropriately queen-sized bed), Lexa meets another widow, plumber Joe's Gina, six years now having passed since his death. She finds herself coerced into constructing a fertility spell for Gina's youngest daughter, Veronica, who has been trying to conceive for the same amount of time. Life, it seems, is not entirely done with the widows, and certainly not done with vital Lexa.

Dealing again with life and death, the witches continue to revisit those who remember them; for example, Sukie meets the once-glorious Tommy Gorton, who had been her lover but now has declined into grizzled, crippled, heavy-gutted middle age. He works for half shares on fishing boats from time to time but really is dependent on his wife, a banker. With grown children of his own, he is "a big sad maimed lummox whose life had amounted to nothing," in Sukie's words (171). Tommy propositions Sukie and then insults and rejects her, partly in fear of the loss of his own marriage and livelihood; nonetheless she characteristically casts a benevolent spell on him, beginning to heal his hand, which is withered as the result of a waterfront accident.

Once death-dealers in Eastwick, the witches now are stalked by a mysterious androgynous stranger (who turns out to be Christopher Gabriel from the earlier novel) and are subjected to unexpected and unnerving electrical shocks. Lexa finds Jane's fearful dramatization of the situation and Christopher's "half-recognized visage . . . so New England, so *Scarlet Letter*" (177), in another tip of the hat to Hawthorne.

The leader of the previous novel's competing coven, musician Greta Neff, who is also now a widow, makes an appearance as well. Pastor Brenda Parsley is gone and all but forgotten, replaced by the overwhelmingly good parson Debbie Larcom, whose body is perfect (reminding of Jenny Gabriel of the earlier novel) but whose sermons seem to be New Age hokum; her texts include Matthew 16:25, "gender-corrected to 'For whosoever will save his or her life shall lose it, and whosoever will lose his or her life shall find it,'" as well as *Self* magazine, *Our Bodies, Our Selves,* and *Webster's New Collegiate Dictionary* (182).

In an attempt to counter the malevolent forces working against them, the three witches once more attempt to raise their cone of power in their condo living room, but in the melodramatic event, Jane is stricken by an aortic aneurysm at the same moment that Sukie casts her healing charm for Tommy, perhaps echoing the principle from the earlier novel that the sacrifice of a life is required to make a spell. Lexa calls 911, and she and Sukie hurriedly clothe Jane and themselves as the EMT unit approaches.

Jane dies in the hospital the next morning, and the witches' link to Eastwick is broken. Lexa and Sukie attend her funeral in Brookline, meeting Jane's ancient and once beautiful mother-in-law—another witch, as it turns out. They sit through a service notable for the inanity of its eulogy (a male friend of Jane's deceased husband manages to work in golfing metaphors, including a hole in one) and the irrelevance of its litany. Chris Gabriel makes an appearance at the cemetery and later reveals himself as the source of the electric shocks that had bedeviled Jane and Lexa. As the novel draws toward its close, his power is diffused, and he moves into Sukie's Manhattan apartment as her kept paramour. Chris eventually melts "back into his half-world, the half he had inherited from Darryl Van Horne" (308), much as the witches' first husbands faded away. Lexa returns to New Mexico, thinking the witching part of her life over, but in the end she makes a phone call to Sukie, who recognizes her voice immediately. The two women reconnect again, ready for more adventures and more travel.

Many reviewers at the time of publication seemed to underestimate *The Widows of Eastwick,* perhaps because they were not reading it in close proximity to its predecessor, on which it riffs continually, following Updike's habit of returning to and reconsidering themes, characters, and settings from previous works. Thus, for example the three sections of *Widows* ("The Coven Reconstituted," "Maleficia [Witchcraft] Revisited," and "Guilt Assuaged") neatly echo and extend the sections of the earlier book ("The Coven," "Maleficia," and "Guilt"). *Widows* is not quite the perfect combination of subject matter, satire, seriousness, and gorgeous writing that *Witches* is, but it comes close and pairs effectively with the earlier novel.

S.

Of the novels directly inspired by *The Scarlet Letter, S.* (1988) is Updike's most straightforward transcription of Hawthorne's characters and situations. It also is funny, perhaps Updike's most accessible comic novel, though it was not well received critically or in terms of sales (Begley 425–26).

The novel's protagonist is the fortyish Sarah Price Worth ("S." for her usual signature), who in April 1986 leaves behind her seaside New England home and cold physician husband (doubling for Hawthorne's Roger Chillingworth) on a quest for personal and spiritual fulfillment. Hester Prynne is an ancestor of Sarah's, if one is to judge from the monogrammed, tarnished family silver (264). Sarah is like Hester, "a figure of perfect elegance on a large scale" (233), and as the novel begins, she is on a jet plane en route to the Arizona commune of Shri Arhat Mindadali, M.A., Ph.D. Updike's fictional commune and the issues and events surrounding it seem closely modeled, perhaps too closely, on the notorious Rajneeshpuram, Oregon, commune of the early 1980s, in keeping with his habit of appropriating recent events into the fabric of his novels. The guru Arhat first engaged Sarah's attention via an inspirational cassette tape she listened to when she was a member of a suburban ladies' yoga group and more interested in secrets of slimming than the mysteries of life. Like the original Hester of Hawthorne's novel, Sarah has a daughter, Pearl, around whom issues of women's place in society similarly coalesce. Sarah's Pearl has left Yale for a year in London, which has devolved into a planned marriage into a Dutch family, perhaps noble in descent but making its money in the present time from brewing, too prosaic a vocation for Sarah's taste. A Radcliffe dropout herself, Sarah objects to this detour from independent female achievement (and Pearl's eventual pregnancy), seeing it as a repetition of the pattern of her own younger self.

Christopher Lehmann-Haupt, in his *New York Times* review of *S.*, wrote, "The unfolding of Sarah's character is a tour de force. Mr. Updike is predictably dazzling in his mimicry of an intelligent, witty, articulate woman with the fullest possible storehouse of gripes and perceptions about the role of women in contemporary America. In fact he seems almost to luxuriate in the persona of Sarah, exploring aspects of her past and personality that go far beyond the practical demands of the plot." Lehmann-Haupt found the novel's portrayal of Sarah misogynistic; after considering whether that view derived from the dour perspective of the protagonist of *Roger's Version,* he decided that the point of view was Updike's own and was not praiseworthy. This assessment perhaps underestimates Updike's comic achievement.

S. is an epistolary novel, a genre that in the late twentieth century has expanded to include transcriptions from cassette tape correspondence and even Sarah's surreptitious recordings of sexual encounters and other interactions among the characters. A good deal of the novel's appeal derives from the varying tones of these letters and tapes, as well as from the alternately savvy and naive narration provided by Sarah as she moves into Arhat's rural Arizona commune. Sarah is renamed Kundalini after "the serpent of female energy dormant at the base of the spinal column" (272), and she rapidly rises from artichoke cultivator to concrete finisher to backhoe operator to typist/stenographer to chief accountant of the Ashram's tangled finances, in the wake of the former accountant's apparent mental breakdown. She also becomes chief concubine. Even the divine Arhat joins the other men in her life as seeming to be more impressed by Sarah's physical charms than her intelligence and personality.

To say that all is not precisely as it seems in the commune is a considerable understatement. Sarah's quest to discover the reality behind life's appearances becomes both a spiritual journey treated seriously by Updike (he even provides a thirteen-page glossary of Buddhist and Hindu terms to testify to his careful research) and a comic series of her personal pratfalls. There is an attempted assault by a spurned lover during a spiritual exercise and ecstatic, tantric sex that abruptly verges into something more appropriate to the three Stooges. The downfall of the commune via violations of zoning and land use laws, excursions into illegal drugs and prostitution, the intentional poisoning of many of the residents, and other peccadilloes echoes the actual Rajneeshpuram commune's fate. At novel's end Sarah is on to new adventures, perhaps not spiritually enlightened by her nine months at the commune but certainly enriched, since she has taken to skimming a considerable portion of the donations received during her tenure as chief accountant. Sarah is apparently the only novice in the short history of the commune not to lose money on her investment in Ashram Arhat.

This novel probably deserved a better reaction than it received; however it compares unfavorably to *The Witches of Eastwick* in skewing too much toward the comic and in so closely paralleling elements of *The Scarlet Letter*. It does not walk the interesting line between satire and seriousness as does *Witches:* the stakes are not as high as in that novel, and so the payoffs are lower. Overall Updike's riffing on Hawthorne's works and themes is most effective in the two Eastwick novels, since in these he most completely rethinks and adapts these themes to the contemporary United States.

CHAPTER 6

Guide to Major Works
The Henry Bech Novellas

The Bech novellas comprise three works, *Bech: A Book* (1970), *Bech Is Back* (1982), and *Bech at Bay: A Quasi-Novel* (1998), which also were collected in *The Complete Henry Bech* (2001). The books take on novelists less adept, prolific, and Protestant than Updike. Bech is endlessly blocked, crassly seeks publicity, and is reduced to murdering his critics—and wins the Nobel Prize for Literature, the award that famously eluded Updike.

These three collections, each appearing more than a decade apart beginning in 1970 (an additional story appears in the 2001 collection), might be thought of as prose analogs to Updike's poetry. They are serious, just as Updike's poems do not really fall into the category of light verse, but they also represent a relaxed side of the author, who seems to feel free to play with ideas, characters, and situations, without much sense that he is straining for effect. He is at his ease exploring Bech, a decidedly second-rate New York Jewish novelist on the make, who allows Updike to tweak the noses of contemporaries and peers as diverse as Bernard Malamud, Norman Mailer, J. D. Salinger, Isaac Bashevis Singer, Philip Roth, and Henry Roth. Christopher Lehmann-Haupt, not a fan of *Couples* (which he thought overwritten), found the first Bech book much more his kind of thing: "'Bech' succeeds marvelously. . . . it contains just the right number of words to serve its ends. One falls into the book and through it and out the other side of it as effortlessly as one might slide through a polished aluminum tube in a funhouse. Yet so much is accomplished. It kids what it sets out to kid, and gets away with it. It creates a character that works as a satirical figure and a good deal more."

Bech allows Updike to explore the heights and depths of the profession of authorship and what he himself might have become absent his considerable talent and work ethic. By middle age Bech ceases to write much, and his income derives from such sources as "sale of a forgotten *Collier's* chestnut to a public-television series promoting Minor Masters of the American Short Story" (*Bech is Back* 90) and dribbling royalties from his Beat publications of the mid-1950s (*Bech at Bay* 114). Late in life he navigates the changing landscape of authorship, including European conglomerate takeovers of American publishing houses and the vagaries of book discussion groups.

Celebrity more than authorship is what Bech comes to pursue, and in spite of a writer's block extending a decade and a half, he yearns for (and surprisingly achieves at last) best seller status and then that one great literary prize that justifies his early promise and years spent in the thankless task of pushing his modest talent up the Sisyphean hill of literary renown. Bech is ever open to what comes his way professionally—for example in the government-sponsored cultural tours of third world countries and visiting writer gigs at colleges that let him play literary lion on a modest scale, repeating motifs in the series. (Affairs with various ladies of various ages are thrown in as lagniappe.)

Bech is a monster of sorts, eventually descending to the successful murder of his chief critic and getting away with it in the story "Bech Noir" in *Bech at Bay*. On the whole, however, he is among the most amiable and human of monsters, a character who would not be appropriate if appearing in Updike's most serious fiction but is a great pleasure to meet with in these works of satirical, sometimes farcical, humor.

CHAPTER 7

A Brief Summing Up

A full consideration of Updike's achievement would require a far longer study than this one, but it is hoped that something of his strengths and characteristic concerns are documented here. Remarkably consistent from his earliest works to his later ones, he considered the American landscape—both literal land- and cityscapes and the internal, psychological landscapes of Americans in the American Century, facing a world of unexpected achievements, challenges, and disappointments as well. Like Rabbit Angstrom, Updike well remembered World War II, the high point of American power and achievement, perhaps with a nostalgia possible only to one who had seen it from the point of view of a child. Like Rabbit he also watched American decline from a nation that had seemed to offer great possibilities, despite the many advances made by citizens previously marginalized and excluded. Updike convincingly showed how those advances resonated negatively for men who previously had ruled society (as in the *Rabbit* books) and also burrowed into the perceptions of those facing discrimination and resisting (as particularly with the women of the Eastwick novels). As a cultural icon, he was awarded high honors yet managed to remain workmanlike and sensible both in person and in print (unlike his slyly portrayed comic doppelgänger, Henry Bech). His characters revel in a secular, sensual world (as in *Couples*) but are not able to forget the nation's optimistic religious past, producing a recurrent ironic and satirical strain that marks almost all his works to greater or lesser degree. Updike entertained his readers with that satirical side but also with a writerly style that is a marvel of evocative beauty and with very serious concerns.

Updike was a cultural ambassador for the nation, a husband and father, a poet, a reviewer, and an art critic. Still he likely will be best remembered for his prose fiction. His short stories may go out of fashion in college anthologies (as indeed has already happened), but the collections and novels will remain on the library shelves, modest in dark blue, tan, pastel pink, gray, red, and green cloth bindings. Somewhere in the heartland a little to the east of Kansas a young man or woman may find them there. If so, Updike's life's ambition will again be realized, his work will float anew to the surface, and by his words he will live.

SELECTED BIBLIOGRAPHY

Primary

Updike, John. *The Afterlife and Other Stories*. New York: Knopf, 1994; London: Hamish Hamilton, 1995.

———. *Americana*. New York: Knopf, 2001; London: Penguin, 2001 (poems).

———. *Assorted Prose*. New York: Knopf, 1965; London: Deutsch, 1965 (essays and reviews).

———. *Bech: A Book*. New York: Knopf, 1970; London: Deutsch, 1970 (novel).

———. *Bech at Bay: A Quasi-Novel*. New York: Knopf, 1998; London: Hamish Hamilton, 1999 (novel).

———. *Bech Is Back*. New York: Knopf, 1982; London: Deutsch, 1983 (novel).

——— and Katrina Kenison, eds. *The Best American Short Stories of the Century*. Boston: Houghton Mifflin, 1999.

———. *Bottom's Dream*. New York, Knopf, 1965 (children's book).

———. *Brazil*. New York: Knopf, 1994; London: Hamish Hamilton. 1994 (novel).

———. *Buchanan Dying*. New York: Knopf, 1974; London: Deutsch, 1974 (play).

———. *The Carpentered Hen and Other Tame Creatures; Poems*. New York: Harper, 1958.

———. *The Centaur*. New York: Knopf, 1963; London, Deutsch, 1963 (novel).

———. *A Child's Calendar*. New York: Knopf, 1965 (children's book).

———. *Collected Poems*. New York: Knopf, 1993; London: Deutsch, 1993.

———. *The Complete Henry Bech*. New York: Knopf, 2001; London: Knopf, 2006.

———. *The Coup*. New York: Knopf, 1978; London, Deutsch, 1979 (novel).

———. *Couples*. New York: Knopf, 1968; London: Deutsch, 1968 (novel).

———. *Couples: A Short Story*. Cambridge, Mass.: Halty Ferguson, 1976.

———. *Due Considerations*. New York: Knopf, 2007; London: Hamish Hamilton, 2007 (essays and reviews).

———. *The Early Stories: 1953–1975*. New York: Knopf, 2003; London: Hamish Hamilton, 2004.

———. *Endpoint and Other Poems*. New York: Knopf, 2009.

———. *Facing Nature*. New York: Knopf, 1985; London: Deutsch, 1986 (poems).

———. *Gertrude and Claudius*. New York: Knopf, 2000; London: Hamish Hamilton, 2000 (novel).

———. *Golf Dreams: Writings on Golf*. New York: Knopf, 1996; London: Hamish Hamilton, 1997.

———. *A Helpful Alphabet of Friendly Objects*. New York: Knopf, 1995.

————. *Higher Gossip.* New York: Knopf, 2011 (essays and criticism).

————. *Hoping for a Hoopoe: Poems by John Updike.* London: Gollancz, 1959 (first British publication of *The Carpentered Hen and Other Tame Creatures*).

————. *Hub Fans Bid Kid Adieu: John Updike on Ted Williams.* New York: Library of America, 2010.

————. *Hugging the Shore.* New York: Knopf, 1983 (essays and reviews).

————. *In the Beauty of the Lilies.* New York: Knopf, 1996 (novel).

————. *Jester's Dozen.* Northridge, Cal.: Lord John, 1984 (poems).

————. *Just Looking.* New York: Knopf, 1989; London: Deutsch, 1989 (essays on art).

————. *Licks of Love: Short Stories and a Sequel, "Rabbit Remembered."* New York: Knopf, 2001; London: Hamish Hamilton, 2001.

————. *Love Factories.* Helsinki: Eurographia, 1993 (short stories).

————. *The Magic Flute.* New York: Knopf, 1962; London: Deutsch, 1964 (children's book).

————. *The Maples Stories.* New York: Knopf, 2009.

————. *Marry Me.* New York: Knopf, 1977; London: Deutsch, 1977 (novel).

————. *Memories of the Ford Administration.* New York: Knopf, 1992; London: Deutsch, 1993 (novel).

————. *Midpoint and Other Poems.* New York: Knopf, 1969; London: Deutsch, 1969.

————. *A Month of Sundays.* New York: Knopf, 1975; London: Deutsch, 1975 (novel).

————. *More Matter.* New York, Knopf 1999; London: Hamish Hamilton, 1999 (essays and criticism).

————. *Museums and Women and Other Stories.* New York, Knopf, 1972; London: Deutsch, 1973.

————. *The Music School: Short Stories.* New York: Knopf, 1966; London: Deutsch, 1967.

————. *My Father's Tears and Other Stories.* New York, Knopf, 2009.

————. *Odd Jobs: Essays and Criticism.* New York: Knopf, 1991; London: Deutsch, 1992.

————. *Of the Farm.* New York: Knopf, 1965; London: Deutsch, 1966 (novel).

————. *Of Prizes and Print.* New York, Knopf 1998.

————. *Olinger Stories: A Selection.* New York: Vintage, 1964.

————. *On Literary Biography.* Columbia: University of South Carolina Press, 1999.

————. *Pigeon Feathers, and Other Stories.* New York: Knopf, 1962; London: Deutsch, 1962.

————. *Picked Up Pieces.* New York: Knopf, 1975; London: Deutsch, 1976 (essays and reviews).

————. *The Poorhouse Fair.* New York: Knopf, 1959; London: Gollancz, 1959 (novel).

————. *Rabbit Angstrom: The Four Novels.* New York: Knopf, 1995; *Rabbit Angstrom: A Tetralogy.* London: Everyman's. 1995.

————. *Rabbit at Rest.* New York: Knopf, 1990; London: Deutsch, 1990 (novel).

————. *Rabbit Is Rich.* New York: Knopf, 1981; London: Deutsch, 1982 (novel).

————. *Rabbit Redux.* New York: Knopf, 1971; London: Deutsch, 1972 (novel).

————. *Rabbit, Run.* New York: Knopf, 1960; London: Deutsch, 1961 (novel).

————. *The Ring.* New York: Knopf, 1964 (children's book).

————. *Roger's Version.* New York: Knopf, 1986; London: Deutsch, 1986 (novel).

————. *The Same Door.* New York: Knopf, 1959; London: Deutsch, 1962 (short stories).

————. *S.* New York: Knopf, 1988; London: Deutsch, 1988 (novel).

————. *Seek My Face*. New York: Knopf, 2002; London: Hamish Hamilton, 2004 (novel).

————. *Self-Consciousness*. New York: Knopf, 1989; London: Deutsch, 1989 (memoir).

————. *Seventy Poems*. New York: Penguin, 1972.

————. *Still Looking*. New York: Knopf, 2005; London: Hamish Hamilton, 2006 (reviews and criticism).

————. *Talk from the Fifties*. Northridge, Cal.: Lord John, 1979 (articles).

————. *Telephone Poles and Other Poems*. New York: Knopf, 1963; London: Deutsch, 1964.

————. *Terrorist*. New York: Knopf, 2006; London: Hamish Hamilton, 2006 (novel).

————. *Too Far to Go*. Greenwich, Conn: Fawcett, 1979 (short stories).

————. *Tossing and Turning*. New York: Knopf, 1977; London: Deutsch, 1977 (poems).

————. *Toward the End of Time*. New York: Knopf, 1997; London: Deutsch, 1998 (novel).

————. *Trust Me*. New York: Knopf, 1987 (short stories).

————. *Verse: The Carpentered Hen and Other Tame Creatures; Telephone Poles and Other Poems*. Greenwich, Conn: Fawcett, 1965.

————. *Villages*. New York: Knopf, 2004; London: Hamish Hamilton, 2005 (novel).

————. *The Widows of Eastwick*. New York: Knopf, 2008 (novel).

————. *The Witches of Eastwick*. New York: Knopf, 1984; London: Deutsch, 1984 (novel).

Secondary

Academy of American Achievement. "John Updike Interview." June 12, 2004 (http://prod loadbalancer-1055872027.us-east-1.elb.amazonaws.com/autodoc/page/updoint-1).

"Authors: View from the Catacombs." *Time*, April 28, 1968, 66–75.

Bailey, Peter J. *Rabbit (Un)Redeemed: The Drama of Belief in John Updike's Fiction*. Madison, N.J.: Farleigh Dickinson University Press, 2006.

Baker, Nicholson. *U & I: A True Story*. New York: Random House, 1991.

Batchelor, Bob. *John Updike: A Critical Biography*. Santa Barbara, Cal.: Praeger, 2013.

Begley, Adam. *Updike*. New York: HarperCollins, 2014. Acclaimed full length biography.

Ben Hassat, Hedda. *Prophets without Vision: Subjectivity and the Sacred in Contemporary American Writing*. Lewisburg, Penn.: Bucknell University Press, 2000.

Bloom, Harold, ed. *Modern Critical Views of John Updike*. New York: Chelsea House, 1987.

Boswell, Marshall. *John Updike's Rabbit Tetralogy: Mastered Irony in Motion*. Columbia: University of Missouri Press, 2001.

Broer, Lawrence. *Rabbit Tales: Poetry and Politics in John Updike's Rabbit Novels*. Tuscaloosa: University of Alabama Press, 2000.

Broyard, Anatole. "Updike's Twosomes." *New Republic*, May 4, 1968, 28–30.

Burchard, Rachel C. *John Updike: Yea Sayings*. Carbondale: Southern Illinois University Press, 1971.

Campbell, Jeff H. *Updike's Novels: Thorns Spell a Word*. Wichita Falls, Tex.: Midwestern State University Press, 1988.

Clarke Taylor, C. *John Updike: A Bibliography*. Kent, Ohio: Kent State University Press, 1968.

Coupland, Douglas. *Generation X: Tales for an Accelerated Culture*. New York: St. Martin's, 1991.

De Bellis, Jack. *John Updike: A Bibliography, 1968–1993*. Westport, Conn.: Greenwood, 1994.

De Bellis, Jack, ed. *John Updike: The Critical Responses to the Rabbit Saga*. Westport, Conn.: Greenwood, 2005.

————. *The John Updike Encyclopedia*, Santa Barbara, Cal.: Greenwood, 2001.

————. *John Updike's Early Years*. Bethlehem, Penn.: Lehigh University Press, 2013.

De Bellis, Jack, and Michael Broomfield. *John Updike: A Bibliography of Primary and Secondary Materials, 1948–2007*. New Castle, Del.: Oak Knoll, 2007.

Detweiler, Robert. *John Updike*. New York: Twayne, 1972; revised, Boston: Twayne, 1984.

Ditsky, John. "Roth, Updike, and the High Expense of Spirit." *University of Windsor Review* 5, no. 1 (1969): 111–20.

Emerson, Ralph Waldo. *Emerson's Nature—Origin, Growth, Meaning*. Ed. Merton M. Sealts, Jr. & Alfred R. Ferguson. New York & Toronto, Dodd, Mead, 1969.

Greiner, Donald. "Don DeLillo, John Updike, and the Sustaining Power of Myth." In *UnderWords: Perspectives on Don DeLillo's Underworld*, edited by Joseph Dewey, Steven G. Kellman, and Irving Malin, 103–13. Newark: University of Delaware Press, 2002.

————. *John Updike's Novels*. Athens: Ohio University Press, 1984.

————. *The Other John Updike: Poems, Short Stories, Prose, Play*. Athens: Ohio University Press, 1981.

Gullette, Margaret Morganroth. "John Updike: Rabbit Angstrom Grows Up." In *Safe at Last in the Middle Years: The Invention of the Midlife Progress Novel*, 58–84. Berkeley: University of California Press, 1988.

Hamilton, Alice, and Kenneth Hamilton. *The Elements of John Updike*. Grand Rapids, Mich.: Eerdmans, 1970.

————. "Metamorphosis through Art: John Updike's *Bech: A Book*." *Queen's Quarterly* 77 (1970): 624–36.

————. "The Validation of Religious Faith in the Writings of John Updike." *Studies in Religion/Sciences Religieuses: A Canadian Journal* 5 (1975) 275–85.

Howard, Jane. "Can a Nice Novelist Finish First?" *Life* 61, no. 19. (Nov. 4, 1966): 74–82.

Hunt, George W. *John Updike and the Three Great Secret Things: Sex, Religion, and Art*. Grand Rapids, Mich.: Eerdmans, 1985.

Jay, Elisabeth. "'Who Are You Gentle Reader?': John Updike—*A Month of Sundays* (1975)." *Literature and Theology* 19, no. 4. (2005): 346–54.

Kakutani, Michiko. "Memory Arpeggios in Updike's Sunset." *New York Times*, May 25, 2009.

Karshan, Thomas. "Batsy." *London Review of Books*, March 31, 2005.

Kingsolver, Barbara. "Desire under the Palms." *New York Times*, February 6, 1994.

Lehmann-Haupt, Christopher. "Books of the Times: Updike: A Mensch." *New York Times*, June 11, 1970.

————. "In John Updike's Latest, the Woman Called 'S.'" *New York Times*, March 7, 1988.

————. "John Updike, a Lyrical Writer of the Middle-Class Man, Dies at 76." *New York Times*, January 28, 2009.

Luscher, Robert M. *John Updike: A Study of the Short Fiction*. New York: Twayne, 1993.

McNaughton, William R., ed. *Critical Essays on John Updike*. Boston: Hall, 1982.

Markle, Joyce B. *Fighters and Lovers: Themes in the Novels of John Updike*. New York: New York University Press, 1973.

Martin, John Stephen. "Rabbit's Faith: Grace and the Transformation of the Heart." *Pacific Coast Philology* 17 (1982): 103–11.

Miller, D. Quentin. *John Updike and the Cold War: Drawing the Iron Curtain*. Columbia: University of Missouri Press, 2001.

Morley, Catherine. "The Bard of Everyday Domesticity: John Updike's Song for America." In *The Quest for Epic in Contemporary American Literature*. New York: Routledge, 2011, 57–83.

Newman, Judie. *John Updike*. London: Macmillan, 1988.

O'Connell, Mary. *Updike and the Patriarchal Dilemma: Masculinity in the Rabbit Novels*. Carbondale: Southern Illinois University Press, 1996.

Olster, Stacey Michele. *The Cambridge Companion to John Updike*. Cambridge: Cambridge University Press, 2006.

Plath, James, ed. *Conversations with John Updike*. Jackson: University Press of Mississippi, 1994.

Pontell, Jonathan. "About Generation Jones." The Jonathan Pontell Group. 2007 (http://web.archive.org/web/20110713115711/http://www.jonathanpontell.com/aboutgenjones.htm).

Porter, M. Gilbert. "John Updike's 'A&P': The Establishment and an Emersonian Cashier." *English Journal* 61, no. 8 (1972): 1155–58.

Pritchard, William H. *Updike: America's Man of Letters*. South Royalton, Ver.: Steerforth, 2000. Revised, Amherst: University of Massachusetts Press, 2005.

Ristoff, Dilvo I. *John Updike's* Rabbit at Rest: *Appropriating History*. New York: Peter Lang, 1998.

Roiphe, Anne. *For Rabbit, with Love and Squalor*. Washington, D.C.: Free Press, 2000.

Searles, George J. *The Fiction of Philip Roth and John Updike*. Carbondale: Southern Illinois University Press, 1984.

Schiff, James A. *John Updike Revisited*. Woodbridge, Conn.: Twayne, 1998.

———. *Updike's Version: Rewriting* The Scarlet Letter. Columbia: University of Missouri Press, 1992.

Singh, Sukhbir. "'Back on to the Life Wagon': An Interview with John Updike." *Irish Journal of American Studies* 5 (1996): 77–91.

———. "Fire, Rain, Rooster: John Updike's Christian Allegory in *Couples*." *International Fiction Review* 23, nos. 1–2 (1996): 36–43.

Tallent, Elizabeth. *Married Men and Magic Tricks: John Updike's Erotic Heroes*. Berkeley, Cal.: Creative Arts Book Company, 1982.

Tanner, Tony. "A Compromised Environment." In *City of Words: American Fiction, 1950–1970*. London: Jonathan Cape, 1971, 273–94.

Thorburn, David, and Howard Eiland, eds. *John Updike: A Collection of Critical Essays*. Englewood Cliffs, N.J.: Prentice-Hall, 1979.

Trachtenberg, Stanley, ed. *New Essays on* Rabbit, Run. Cambridge: Cambridge University Press, 1993.

Trilling, Diana. "Updike's Yankee Traders." *Atlantic Monthly*, April 1968, 129–31.

Uphaus, Suzanne H. *John Updike*. New York: Ungar, 1980.

Vidal, Gore. "Rabbit's Own Burrow: The Comfortable Patriotism of John Updike and His Fiction." *Times Literary Supplement*, April 26, 1996.

Wallace, David Foster. "John Updike, Champion Literary Phallocrat, Drops One; Is This

Finally the End for Magnificent Narcissists?" *New York Observer*, 12 October 1997.

Wood, James. "Gossip in Gilt." *London Review of Books,* 19 April 2001.

———. "John Updike's Complacent God." In *The Broken Estate: Essays on Literature and Belief.* New York: Modern Library, 2000, 249–72.

Yerkes, James. *John Updike and Religion: The Sense of the Sacred and the Motions of Grace.* Grand Rapids, Mich.: Eerdmans, 1999.

INDEX